RETROVENTURISM

Business Law, EPCOT, and Building a Brighter Tomorrow

Richard A.C. Alton

Retroventurism: Business Law, EPCOT, and Building a Brighter Tomorrow is the first Project Law eXperimental book.

ISBN 978-0-578-83548-8

Special thanks to my wife Melissa for supporting me as I researched and wrote into the night. A thank you as well to Sean who was my springboard for ideas. Also a debt owed to Kayla and David for their edits and thoughts. A final thank you to Chloe for the thoughtful design work.

Contents

Introduction
Retroventurism and Project Law eXperimental

O ne of my favorite aspects of the writing of Charles Dickens is when he speaks to you in his work. Not just as any author speaks to their reader in that general "I wrote this" sense, but Dickens actually speaks to you. It is as if, and to take his words, he is standing at your elbows while you read. The book therefore is an extension of himself. This literary device is called authorial intrusion, and I love it. In that tradition, here I am, standing in the same spot, speaking to you. Pleasure to meet you. Hopefully, you do not mind as we take this journey together. We will learn together, as well. You may not know it, but you are going to be helping me.

How, you might ask? Well, obviously, if you purchased this book you already helped me, and thank you for that. More than that, if you explore, study, or discuss the ideas in this book, you will leave imprints in the world. Those imprints are like dandelion seeds that will spread out into the wind. My ideas, which are then melded with your ideas, will fly out into the world and plant new ideas for others to spread. In fact, you are the most important part of this book (I will pause while you take a bow). You are what will convert this tome into more than a book. This is our Project Law eXperimental, and I cannot wait to see what you, and those who follow you, contribute to these ideas!

Retroventurism and Project Law eXperimental grew out of my interest in a creation that has had many names: Project X, Project Future, Progress City, the City of the Future, the Reedy Creek Drainage District, the Reedy Creek Improvement District, the Experimental Prototype Community of Tomorrow (EPCOT), or as you may know it … Walt Disney World Resort in Orlando, Florida. A supremely unique business arrangement existing in both the flesh and written word in Florida provides us with an excellent framework for studying business law. This book is both a narrative and an instruction manual. It engages in a bit of historiography (retelling of history in narrative form) and serves as a medium to understanding elements of business law. An additional element, however, a part that gives this book a further nuance, is that it also can be used as an instruction manual on the creation of a business law course or personal study exercise.

There are many aspects of the life of Walt Disney and the creation of the Disney company that could equally serve as a guidebook to business law, but the utterly unique nature of the creation of the Walt Disney World Resort in Orlando truly makes it the best choice in fleshing out business law topics. Business formation, ethics, regulation, business planning, private vs. governmental development, and corporate growth can all be examined through the lens of Walt Disney's Florida land purchase and the subsequent creation of Walt Disney World.

Prior to continuing I want to touch a bit on language. I try my best to use "Walt" when signifying the man, and "Disney" when signifying the company. This is an important distinction, and one that grows as we continue along our journey. For example, I will discuss Walt's brother Roy Disney, and as it is common fashion to refer to individuals by their last name, you can understand the probability of confusion. As such, when you see the word "Disney," I am referring to the business entity, not Walt nor his brother, specifically.

As part and parcel of Project Law eXperimental, during the chapters that follow, you will see sections noted as "eXperimental Tip," which help dive into legal and other deep-think topics. These are useful introspection tools I developed or thought of over the years and either used in class or for my own personal edification. These eXperimental Tips ask you to take this venture one step further, and I fully encourage you to do so. If this book is to be used in a classroom setting, these make for great separate learning adventures. If this book is for personal use, these eXperimental Tips can be used to really delve into the topic and formulate your own opinions. The eXperimental Tips contain suggestions for further reading and list items for exploration. The tips will help enrich your experience reading and really bring Project Law eXperimental to life as you explore these topics!

So, why EPCOT? Where did my fascination with this topic come from? I found during my research many individuals interested in EPCOT have a fascination with the future, science fiction, urban planning, history, education, and, most obvious, Walt Disney and Disney World. It made me wonder, Why was I so fascinated? I did go to EPCOT Center when I was two years old, but it would be almost thirty years later until I returned. It is interesting though, because from time to time I would think upon that picture of me standing in front of that big silver golf ball that is Spaceship Earth. But was that the reason? I have always had an affinity for science fiction, especially *Star Trek*, in all of its iterations. I am not a full-blown Trekkie, but I am close enough. I also loved playing SIM City as a kid. I remember it was one of the first computer games I ever spent hours, even stretching late into the night, playing. I am also interested in history and discovering the past. I have a vague recollection of searching online to find out what EPOCT meant, and then I ran across the Experimental Prototype Community of Tomorrow. My mind was blown, and I was driven to find out more. Having said all that, it makes me wonder where your interest in this book came from. Are the reasons the same as mine or something completely different?

As far as my desire to combine my interest in EPCOT and business law, I started to form an interest in EPCOT's history in between the second and third time I taught business law at the associates degree level. I was searching for a new final project to assign to my students. My first time teaching the course I had them do business plans, as I liked working on business plans as an attorney. But I found out many of my students were required to do business plans for their other classes, so I needed something new. My second time teaching, I had them break out into small groups for their final project for which they had to research and argue a case before a mock court. This is a similar process used in law schools called moot court competitions. It was fun, and the students and administration liked it, but the reality was my students were not taking this class to become lawyers (though skills in researching and presenting an opinion in an orderly manner are good for those interested in business); they were taking the class to earn degrees in business administration, travel and tourism, international business management, and communications. I wanted to find something that brought them closer to home but was not another business plan ... EPCOT! That's it! I would have them argue for the creation of an EPCOT they developed. They would make a presentation at the end of the semester to go along with a written portion. The fact is Disney's Florida property and its special district status serve as such a fascinating link between business and government that the topic is perfect for a business law class.

I would introduce my students midway through the semester to the history behind the Experimental Prototype Community of Tomorrow via a PowerPoint presentation. This presentation would include two main portions; (1) the EPCOT Film; and (2) My own general background on the Florida land purchase, definition of a special district, and the overview of the rights afforded to Disney. The presentation would be used to help my students focus on what their final project would be. That PowerPoint is also the genesis for this book, as I would break off into tangents about each of the topics, such as Walt's secret companies or how the Disney company did actually incorporate some items of the EPCOT Film into Walt Disney World itself (these became eXperimental Tips). You ready for my latest presentation? Let us see how this main sail sets!

CHAPTER 1
The Law of Business: The Eye for an Eye Test

So, how does the American Revolution and a black stone stele from the depths of history fit together as means of laying the foundation of legal relationships developed under commerce? Quite nicely, I believe. This chapter reaches into the past to help formulate what it means when we say *business law*. Piercing out this understanding will give us more solid footing moving forward as we explore retroventurism and Walt's plans for Florida in later chapters. Although, not to leave Disney totally out of this chapter, you should know this is my own personal homage to my favorite ride at Walt Disney World's Epcot theme park: Spaceship Earth. So, if you are reading this, well you can thank the Phoenicians.

While I cannot take you on a physical journey through our collective past as the ride Spaceship Earth does, I will do my best to illustrate meaningful highpoints as we go along a historical path of how we now regulate businesses. These touchstones build upon each other to create the foundation for modern day business law. Before we dip into ancient history, let us pause in the present and take a look at what business law means in the current academic setting.

Business law courses are taught to educate students about the laws surrounding people's interactions with and through business. These courses can cover immense ground. In law schools, business law courses are usually broken up to give students a more in-depth examination of particular elements of business law. For undergrad programs, business law is taken as a collective course and immerses students into the generalities of people and their commercial matters.

An undergrad course on business law covers a gamut of topics that, when combined, move us towards answering the ultimate question: "What is business law?" These topics include: legal theory, foundational statutes, court systems, criminal law, civil litigation, property law, torts, contract law, agency, business formation, governance, employment law, environmental law, insurance, cyber law, international law, consumer protection, intellectual property, alternative dispute resolution, administrative law, and the Uniform Commercial Code. Each of these topics can be found as separate courses in business or law schools. This list is neither exhaustive nor final, as many realms of business law can be partitioned out of these and new ones are being created every day. This illustrates just how broad business law is as a topic and can be as a course.

As we explore what is commonly referred to as *business law*, it is perhaps equally, if not more, constructive to look at each word individually. *Business* deals with a person entering the grand river that is the commerce stream. While one can be in business for the themselves, they cannot create a functioning business without the impact of others, like customers for example. A business generally means the operation of service or the sale of product for another's benefit or enjoyment—at a price, of course! Terms like *professions, trade*, and *career* are intrinsically tied to a person's operation of, or in, a business. Questions such as "Do you own a business?" harken more to a business as a separate entity, something apart from the individual, and that is worth delving into prior to jumping into what is *law*.

Businesses as a form, as something apart from the person running the business, have historical prototypes in ancient India with the advent of *sreni* (organizations that could independently own land and conduct business) and during the Song Dynasty in China (circa 960 C.E.) with the creation of partnerships and stock companies that could engage separately and independently in business. In America, we find businesses with roots in the trading companies established by European sovereigns for business ventures across the Atlantic. Business entities also began to grow domestically in the American Colonies as licensed directly or indirectly by the English Crown. Such early establishments included The New York Company, used to establish fisheries, and The Philadelphia Contributionship, established for home insurance against fire. With the advent of the American Revolution, the nature of business entities required new fashioning in the burgeoning United States. Whereby, North Carolina took the first leap by offering to the general public the ability to incorporate a business for the creation of canals. It was now open season on incorporation.[1]

Law, however, has a much longer existence than businesses as a separate form. Law, in its most general sense, is how a community structures the interaction between its members and the need to enforce community standards. In this sense, law has existed since the first breaths of communal living. When our ancestors began to conglomerate in cities, they realized that to have a functioning civil society, as opposed to an arbitrary amalgamation of ideals, it would behoove them to set some ground rules.

Many early ground rules seemed almost a given, as similar rules appear across many early cultural groupings. Rules such as *Do not kill your neighbor*

---

1 The freshly formed North Carolina government also granted these new corporations the right of eminent domain, or the ability to seize land from another in exchange for market value. That is an interesting right to grant to a private party.

or *Do not steal*, for example. The connectedness across multiple cultures to these base rules is intriguing. It is almost as if some of these early rules are universally true for all people (lucky for you this is not a philosophy or religious studies book, or we would be on the topic of universal truth for the next thousand years). Eventually, as time progressed, those ground rules became written laws. One of our earliest examples of written law comes in the form of Hammurabi's Code, the old eye for an eye!

Hammurabi's Code is a collection of laws reportedly enacted by the Babylonian King Hammurabi (reign circa 1792–1750 BCE) for his empire located in what is now modern-day Iraq. This collection of laws is much more than its most famous line. *Eye for an eye* references that if someone stabs your eye out, the law requires your apparent archnemesis to have an eye removed in equal retribution for his crime against you. In fact, there are close to 300 laws in Hammurabi's Code. These laws cover various rules and regulations, including murder, battery, family law, agriculture, and building practices. Yet the importance of Hammurabi's Code, beyond its completeness and age, is that it is a written law code.

A written law code is a great equalizer; it removes the arbitrary decision-making element from the ruling elite and thus encourages, whether actual or not, a sense of accountability against those same elites as well as the greater society as a whole. An ancient Babylonian knew the rules of the game, what was allowed and what would happen if she broke those rules. She knew where she could go to seek redress for wrongs done against her or her loved ones, and how to prove she was wronged. A written law code sets the stage of societal interaction while also aiming to set limits on abuse of power (in a relative sense, of course; elites are always going to act elitist).

eXperimental Tip: Over 3,500 years have passed, but some things never change. Hammurabi's Code is a great tool to begin to understand the history of written laws and also explore the foundational elements of law. The laws contained in Hammurabi's Code are easy to follow and thus give a great base understanding as to why societies develop laws and what laws early civilizations deemed important. In Hammurabi's Code, these foundational elements extend beyond "eye for an eye." An exploration of Hammurabi's Code unfolds ideas of false testimony (Laws #1–3), personal injury valuation (the vast references to silver, gold, minas, and shekels as a reimbursements for bodily injury or medical costs, specific examples include Laws #209, 211, 213 & 215–217), construction law & premises liability (Laws #228, 229 & 233), judicial accountability (Law #5), and the list goes on and on. Feel free to search for the complete list of Hammurabi's Code and investigate these laws. What other connections can be drawn between these laws and our modern-day statutes? If you were designing a code of law, what would be your top ten laws?

Hammurabi's Code focused both on personal and commercial activities. It is in those commercial activities that we begin to see the formation of business transactions within ancient laws. Laws regulating commercial activities began to take on more importance when more individuals became reliant on trade and commerce for their survival and wants. For example, ancient Greeks, who produced much if not almost all of their daily necessities and wants in their own homes, had much less need for commercial regulations than the average city dweller today who needs to purchase most if not all of their wants and needs from others. Regulations focusing on commerce usually began to develop out of need and utilization of third parties in a transaction. A few fantastic examples from history are *money changers*, *translators*, and *market stalls*.

Money changers began to appear in the fairs and markets of ancient Babylonians and Phoenicians, setting the foundation for our modern international banking systems. But some of the most famous money changers in history are also famous for having a bad day. As recounted in the New Testament portion of the Bible, Jesus—in what has been called either the "Temple Tantrum" or the "Cleansing of the Temple"—visits the famous Temple of Jerusalem, where therein proceeds to knock over the money changers' tables. The basis for doing this is debated by theologians and scholars. As Professor James McGrath notes, the presence of money changers at the Temple of Jerusalem was not seen as defilement of the Temple as it has been portrayed, but rather as a requirement so that visitors to the Temple could exchange their own form of currency to Tyrian Shekels, the required form of Temple tax payments. The knocking over of the tables is more of a symbolic act rather than a judgment being passed on business activities on the Temple grounds.

Translators find a historical connection to a Greek god. According to the polyglot Alex Gross, the ancient Greek word for translator was *hermêneus*, which is directly related to the name of the Greek god Hermes. The word also had many meanings—mediator, go-between, deal-broker, marriage-broker.

Translators also find traction in the Roman Republic, whereby evidence of translators moving into roles of business brokers between the Romans and Carthaginians can be seen in the first treaty between those two states. A business broker is one that arranges a business deal between two parties and, in theory, the broker may represent one party or neither party, merely acting as a faciliatory. As time progresses, we can see the translator assumed a larger role, fostering and connecting business transactions when needed. Which makes sense, as cross-cultural international trade began to take place at higher levels and with more frequency.

Further in time, we arrive at the medieval market stalls. In these markets, we find medieval European cities setting up protectionist measures, whereby local farmers and producers would be allowed to open their market stalls in town earlier than traveling foreign merchants, a sort of encouragement to buy local. This may not seem like much, but it is an interesting aspect of early business regulation. These types of restrictions are the forebearers to towns regulating business hours and controlling the issuance of business licenses or permits. Importantly, the arrival of foreign merchants into medieval European markets also brought knowledge. Arabic trade influence into Europe cannot be underestimated in the impact of modern commercial law, with the advent of such common business terms as *tariff*, *average*, and *check* having origins in the Arabic language.[2]

Strict control over these market stalls, translators, and money changers would take time to develop, as would the many other early understandings of the rules regarding commercial transactions. These early regulations mostly fell under the umbrella of *customary law* or usage. *Customary law* is, at its base, what it says, a law based upon customs of the past as opposed to written law. Even in custom the roots are there for what will eventually become codified, or recorded, business laws. One move directly linked to the rise of codified business laws was the use of recorded transactions and accountings, especially those on the international level.

The ancient Phoenicians developed an alphabet system that would, in effect, make trade, recording transactions, and accounting easier with the new cultures they interacted with. The need to find a mutual way to record transactions in various languages arose as the Phoenicians developed a trading empire around the Mediterranean Sea (1200 B.C.E. to 800 B.C.E). Their alphabet consisted of about twenty-two letters. As they traversed the Mediterranean, their alphabet sailed along with them. The Phoenicians and their trading partners would use this alphabet to record transactions in hopes

---

2 A fun one I just discovered is "fella." *Fellah* is the Arabic word for peasant. But fella in English is presumably derived as a colloquial use of the longer "fellow." However, I now wonder if that is true and if "Hey, fella!" actually should trace its roots to Arabic. Maybe you can help find the answer.

of avoiding something getting lost in translation. The Phoenician alphabet would go on to form the basis of the Greek, Aramaic, and Etruscan writing systems. Thus the writing systems of Latin and all languages derived from Latin, including the major languages of Europe.

Taking a leap to the near past, the development of commerce between nations rapidly increased during the past several hundred years. During this time, we see an increase in uniform laws between all nations. These laws interestingly found a push not only from the top down (i.e. the ruling elite pushing regulations onto their citizens), but also from the bottom up. Whereby merchants, manufacturers, wholesalers, shippers, producers, and brokers craved uniformity and stability, the rise of written agreements, especially those focused on the production and transport of goods over vast areas, gave rise to the law of contracts. In doing so, business law continued to take shape into its modern form.

This brings us to the modern area. Doing an internet search for the definition of business law is a fun activity, as you will be inundated with responses such as: business law, also known as commercial law, also known as mercantile law, also known as trade law. While it is fun to see so many names, tracking down a precise definition is not an essential element to understanding and exploring all that business law has to offer. Appreciating the grand nature of business law is what forged this chapter into its current form. Thus, we are now equipped with basic historical understandings of what business law means as we have ridden along our path through time.

Business law touches so many aspects of law and our lives in general. Isaac A. Hourwich notes it beautifully in his early 1900s article when he states, "[T]o define the boundaries of one particular science without trespassing upon neighboring ground in this day of mutual interdependence among all branches of human knowledge is a task of some difficulty." In short, a term can mean much and more. Siphoning a specific definition is not important. To take the words of one famous judge when speaking of a very delicate topic, you'll know business law when you see it.

CHAPTER 2
Retroventurism

Is retroventurism a made-up word? Yes, but in the words of Thor from the *Avengers* movie, "all words are made up." It took a new word to really get at what I aimed to do with this work. This book utilizes Walt's Experimental Prototype Community of Tomorrow (i.e. EPCOT) concept and the Disney company's Florida land purchase as a means of teaching and learning about business law. In developing a pathway to link these topics, EPCOT and business law, I began to notice a pattern of activity used not only by myself but others as well. This methodology and pathway had no name, though. I needed a word that captured the essence of what I was encountering. So, I invented "retroventurism," combining *retro* for an imitation of style, *venture* for a daring undertaking, and *ism* for a system.[3]

Retroventurism has two forms: theoretical and practical. Theoretical retroventurism researches past unfulfilled business models and imagines what it would be like if they had been completed per the specifications of their original creator. Practical retroventurism is taking the road maps of past business models and re-imagining their utility to create a brand-new enterprise in the spirit of, but not in the strict adherence to, the past model. In terms of business, retroventurism is the soil in which the flower of inspiration grows.

Retroventurism captures the idea of learning from the past while focusing on creating a brighter tomorrow. Retroventurism is a means of tapping into the all-important mental vehicle for change: inspiration. Inspiration is defined as being mentally stimulated to do something. Inspiration itself is the foundation of creation. Although, inspiration for a brighter tomorrow must come from somewhere. One place where that somewhere resides is the unfulfilled yesterday.

Dr. Martin Luther King duly proclaimed, "one of the great agonies of life is that we are constantly trying to finish that which is unfinishable." There is something that innately draws us into completing the dreams of others as a recognition of this human condition for incompleteness. In doing so, we ask two very important questions: "What if?" and even more compelling, "What

---

3 The term retrofuturism helped give birth to the name retroventurism. Retrofuturism is as it sounds, an exploration of past versions of the future. In its most notable form, the origin of the word relates back to a 1984 review of the movie *Brazil*. Retrofuturism is futurism tinged with nostalgia, as it is an interest in the way the future was supposed to be. Some examples include a future based on Art Deco stylings or Jules Verne controlled future scape.

now?" We can learn so much about the trials and tribulations of past business plans, learn from their failures, and build upon their successes to build a brighter tomorrow. Are you ready to join me on our journey to tomorrow? I have been waiting just for you.

What is the central venture we are using in the book? What does EPCOT mean? Why was Disney's Florida land purchase so special and unique? What was Walt's dream for EPCOT? What impact did Walt's death have on that dream? I begin to lay the foundations for all this and more. In addressing these items lies my hope of building the groundwork for future designs and aspirations, not only of mine, but of others and yours as well. To begin unpacking all of this, we will need to take a trip back in time to explore not only when Walt Disney first envisioned EPCOT, but also visions of other luminaries who sought to conjure a brighter future.

The histories that lay before us in this chapter settle the foundation for the pages that are yet to come. Here we meet Walt Disney himself and learn about his vision for a Community of Tomorrow. We are also introduced to artists, urban planners, inventors, writers, and real estate developers. All these individuals have a role to play in this book, some more than others, and none more than Walt himself. This was a fun chapter for me, as first and foremost I am a student of history. Let us meet these visionaries and their visions, starting with Walt Disney.

When I generally speak of Epcot (notice the slight difference in capitalization), undoubtedly thoughts of theme parks and Walt Disney World Resort come to your mind. Maybe you are even familiar with Spaceship Earth, the giant silver ball that makes its home in the Epcot theme park. Yet Walt Disney's original EPCOT (all caps again) was something entirely different, it was a vision of the future, a dream so delicate one says if you tried to grasp it, it may fall apart in your hands. But let us try anyway…

By the early 1960s, Walt Disney was riding a wave of success with Disneyland and a well-established, healthy, and thriving movie studio. Walt even designed and built new film and art studio complexes for the Disney company and helped design a college campus at California Institute of the Arts. But all of this had been in Southern California. Upon the success and draw of Disneyland, Walt was pulled by internal and external focuses to bring his theme parks east of the Mississippi and, in fact, all over the world. Discussions for a St. Louis hybrid location were held, and New York would soon be featuring Disney-designed pavilions at the upcoming World's Fair. The eyes of the Disney theme park world were trending towards the eastern United States. It was not so much a question of, Would he? but, Where would he? There was a draw, and that draw as we now know would lead eventually to Florida.

Was the plan always to build Disneyland East, banking upon the success of Disneyland, in California? One would be hard pressed to deny that would not be a good idea to do. However, as Walt once opined himself, he was not a sequels man. He wanted to be ahead of the curve and not rest on his laurels. Walt also picked up a remarkably interesting hobby over his years of film production and theme park creation—that of urban planning. His reworking of his own film studios taught him how to best address issues facing how people work. His innovative design work for Disneyland, which included the movement of massive amounts of people in a contained area and the development and implementation of new transportation systems, such as the Monorail, taught him how to design places for people to have fun (and hopefully learn something while doing so). Walt formulated a campus and created a layout to harmonize how people learn with his work at CalArts. He now wanted to combine those three—work, fun, and study—with one more element: how to live. Thus the Experimental Prototype Community of Tomorrow, or EPCOT (all caps), was born.

As we work later in chapters, we delve into the original and changing ideals of EPCOT under both Walt Disney and, later, his successors. In those chapters to come, I use various stages of the narrative of Walt and the Disney company's experiences in Florida to explore specific elements of business law and retroventurism. To help us explore retroventurism in particular, we need to explore history. It will be beneficial as we proceed along our path, and in doing so I can give you a taste of what EPCOT was meant to be in addition to offering some other interesting historical tidbits.

The 1950s and 1960s were a time of interest in "tomorrow" and "beyond." Visionary leaders like Dr. Martin Luther King, Jr. were beginning to use terms like "cosmic significance" in church sermons. King was not alone in looking beyond the current earthly outlook. I am going to focus on a few unique individuals from this time period to help us grasp this fascination with the future. Yet it should be noted, ideas of the future are nothing new, of course. Earlier in the century we have the origins of a movement called futurism.

We actually have an Italian born in Egypt to thank for futurism itself. Futurism was launched by the Italian poet and artist Filippo Tommaso Marinetti in 1909. In his move towards futurism, Marinetti stressed a desire to free Italy from its "innumerable museums which cover her like countless cemeteries." Futurists idealized an art that celebrated the modern world of industry and technology. Futurism incorporated this ideology through writing and the arts with a focus on inventiveness, modernity, industrial speed, disruptiveness, and an energetic brashness. You can see the connection between futurism and the themes EPCOT proposed, such as utilization of industry and technology, and its forward-looking mentality.

> **eXperimental Tip:** A world of fascists clamoring for their own visions of the future! Is this a tale from World War II, maybe the theme of a dystopian novel set in a not-so-distant future? Strangely, no. It is a representation of the dark underbelly of futurism. Futurism has its roots in a fascination not only with the celebration of the modern world but with Italian fascism. Filippo Marinetti, as well as numerous Italian futurists who followed his example, fully embraced militaristic nationalism, which meant Italian fascism. There was a focus on the beauty of a brash modern industrial war machine swarming over Italy's enemies that appealed to the followers of futurism, almost as a verification of their beliefs in modernity. Marinetti himself proffered the idea of fascism being the result of futurism, and this garnered attention from Mussolini, upon whom Marinetti sought to impinge himself. Now as modern Futurist Rose Eveleth notes, "Today, when we talk about futurism, we're not usually talking about sculpture, painting, or poetry. Futurists today are scenario builders, people with advanced degrees in strategic foresight, science fiction writers, consultants to businesses." So, while we can divest the generic futurism from fascism, we should not ignore that there was once a connected root. As Eveleth aptly states, "[t]here are lessons to be learned for today's technologists and futurists in Marinetti's manifesto, and it would be foolish to ignore them."

Moving to the 1950s and 1960s, the first tale I want to cover is of an artistic visionary much forgotten by time who died alone with his works burned by his former partner. Yet this visionary was once one of the most popular cartoonists of his time. His visions of the future were seen by millions, and no one can truly measure the impact he had. Who was this person? Let's meet cartoonist and futurist, Arthur Radebaugh.

During World War II, Arthur Radebaugh designed armored cars and artillery for the U.S. military. After the war, he went to Detroit where he was Chief of the Army's Industrial Design Branch. Arthur eventually moved into the private sector and was an artist for car companies prior to the onset and wide use of photography in automobile marketing. Forced out of a career, Arthur moved towards illustration and launched a Sunday cartoon strip "Closer Than We Think," which ran from 1958 to 1963. It was immensely popular in both the U.S. and Canada, reaching close to 20 million readers at its peak. It was so popular, Radebaugh became known as "The Imagineer."[4]

Some of his images have been collected and pieces of Arthur's work restored. There is even a documentary made about Arthur's life called *Closer Than We Think*. Radebaugh illustrated items that came to fruition, such as warehouses stocked by robots, watches that served as televisions, electric and driverless cars, job interviews being conducted through screens, laser surgery, voice recognizing cash registers for shopping, and wall-to-wall televisions. Things that are not so odd to us now. He also illustrated societal items, such as the use of the massive community surveillance and the police state, as well as home computers being used for teaching. In his comic strip, he ventured to interesting aims, such as illustrating the use of "happy gas" by alien invaders, circle runways for planes that acted like slingshots. Additionally, Arthur drew several items that are important when discussing EPCOT; Arthur dabbled in rejuvenated downtowns, industrial farming, and a city called Motopia, which, unlike the name seems to imply, actually referenced the removal of cars from pedestrian areas and the use of motorized walkways. I want you to keep these last ones in mind as we learn about EPCOT.

When Radebaugh died mostly unrecognized in a Veterans hospital in 1974, his work had been largely forgotten over time (and much of his personal work burned by his ex-partner) and eclipsed by such attractions as Walt Disney's Tomorrowland. But Arthur's use of grounded common forms of futuristic life, such as home entertainment, helped deliver a message to his readers. Radebaugh was able to predict so many inventions because his focus on the needs and desires of everyday people were done in a functional sense. How much of his ideas permeated society at the time is immeasurable. As author and blogger Matt Novak notes, "Radebaugh helped shape mid-century American expectations for what the future held."

For our second tale, I want you to imagine the creative forces that would be forged by a person who survived not just one plane crash, but three. Those forces would compel a man to launch a hundred spaceships and fashion a person whose impulse for a more honest future would impact generations. During the 1960s, we saw the birth of one of the longest lasting television

---

4 For Disney fans, this word may sound familiar, as it is a term used by Disney to describe their own innovative staff members. Interestingly, this term actually comes from a time before Radebaugh with the company Alcoa Aluminum that coined the term "Imagineering." In 1989, Disney filed for a trademark for "Imagineering," claiming first use in 1962.

franchises: *Star Trek*. *Star Trek*, in its various forms over the past sixty years, follows the adventures of the Starship Enterprise and similar star vessels as they trek across the galaxy, visiting planets and space stations and discovering an endless array of new alien species. The initial series of *Star Trek* and the subsequent *Star Trek: The Next Generation* owe their direct creation to an innovative storyteller, Gene Roddenberry.

As Gene relates in a 1966 interview discussing his impetus behind the *Star Trek* series, "Science fiction?[5] Absolutely not. Rather, real adventure in tomorrow's space. Based upon the best scientific knowledge and estimates of what our astronauts of the future may face when they move out of our own solar system and into the vastness of our galaxy." Gene also knew something that I believe Walt Disney would appreciate if not outright articulate himself, as Gene said:

> Star Trek started with the premise that the American television audience is a lot more intelligent and perceptive than the so-called "experts" insist. We feel you can short-change that audience only at your own peril. Thus our people, our vessel, everything seen and heard, must seem honest, real, and as totally believable. As if we were watching detectives, cowboys, interns, or any other "accepted" TV entertainment.

Gene gave the audience due consideration. He had no way of knowing that thoughtfulness would pave the way for six decades of stories of the crew of the Starship Enterprise.

A quick note on Gene himself; prior to developing *Star Trek*, he was a decorated World War II pilot, a police officer, and a plane crash investigator. The last bit is interesting, as he survived three plane crashes himself. American Cartoonist Matthew Inman poetically notes about Gene, "Roddenberry saw life's ephemeral nature lit up against a backdrop of stars." Gene Roddenberry sought to make his life count in inspiring others. He is widely recognized as a visionary for his time, with credit given from such science fiction gurus as George Lucas, creator of *Star Wars*. As we move forward in chapters, I want you to keep Roddenberry's words about creating something "totally believable" in your mind as we talk about how Walt Disney crafted his parks and how he hoped to craft EPCOT.

---

5 Science fiction is a form of fiction that looks toward imagined futures, parallel universes, or technological advances and the stories that evolve from such incursions into the imagination or space. It has as its possible root origin a second century Greek speaking Assyrian named Lucian of Samosata. Although Lucian was a satirist, his work, A True Story, contains travel to outer space, aliens, and interplanetary warfare. Pretty cool!

eXperimental Tip: There is something about both Gene Roddenberry and Arthur Radebaugh's work that runs through a similar stream beyond the futuristic aspect, and that is their recognition of people's desire. Think back on Gene Roddenberry's advice about short-changing the audience. It is such an important consideration in storytelling. Gene acknowledged the significance of the audience's desire for truthfulness even in fiction. This is true as well for Arthur's cartoon strip, and it may be why we see correlations between a 1950s comic strip and modern inventions. Future inventions may not have been based directly off of Arthur's (though I believe they may have indirectly), it may be that Arthur understood what people would really want in their lives. What can you learn from individuals like Radebaugh and Roddenberry about delivering messages of the future? Is it just as important to grasp the human elements inside of the science fiction as much as it is the fantasy? What are some items you think people want in their future?

Special note: There is an interesting correlation between Radebaugh's title of his comic "Closer Than We Think" and the warning in wing mirrors in U.S. automobiles "OBJECTS IN MIRROR ARE CLOSER THAN THEY APPEAR." It may be unrelated, but it is interesting that Arthur worked in automobile advertising. I was trying to ascertain when the warning was required to be put on cars, but to no avail. Let me know if you find out.

EPCOT, as originally planned by Walt, was to be a showcase city of corporate ingenuity, essentially a themed city of intuition, invention, innovation, and implementation. Walt wanted to bring the best and brightest ideas from American companies and put them on display in an entirely self-contained, self-sufficient city. A place where guests from around the world could come visit and see how people of that day and age could be living with the most recent and upcoming advances in art, science, and technology. Walt wanted to remove individuals' reliance on the automobile as well and envisioned transportation hubs to service residents and visitors. As far as the overall initial vision of EPCOT, Walt did eventually succumb to the advice of close companions, including his brother Roy, about actually building another theme-park to give the people what they wanted in addition to offering what Walt felt they needed. Walt would acquiesce to a Disneyland in the East, but his heart and his eye were to be on the creation of the Community of Tomorrow.

Like Radebaugh and Roddenberry, Walt would be telling a story with EPCOT, the story of today's innovations leading to a better tomorrow. Walt understood the impact of theme creation and storytelling beyond the realm of animation. This understanding is best illustrated by his first theme park, Disneyland. Walt's fascination with displaying stories of the past, present, and tomorrow was exemplified in Disneyland. Disneyland was a theme-based theme park, meaning the rides and attractions held underlying stories and were not just enjoyable, fascinating, or exhilarating rides. The initial themes in Disneyland were Adventureland, Frontierland, Fantasyland, Tomorrowland, and Main Street USA.

Disneyland itself was a modern marvel in the realm of people movement. So much work went into moving individuals from themed area to themed area and all the respective rides therein. Walt received immense praise on the functionality of his park designs from well recognized urban planners of his day.

Walt Disney begun researching urban development and city planning in the lead up to EPCOT. He became a fan of the Garden City movement and such urban redesigns that took place in cities like Stockholm, Sweden. Some European cities utilized newly constructed high-density satellite centers outside of the main original city center. These satellites were built with a mix of residential and commercial use, containing transit nodes that could easily propel the citizens back to the main city center and onto other satellite centers. These redesigns, done outside of city centers, sought to offer residents the full accompaniment of commercial enterprises, leisure, and employment without the need to leave the satellite area. This may seem familiar to you reading today, but during the beginning half of the twentieth century, the ideas were thought of as revolutionary.

All of this newfound interest of Walt's centers around what is termed as urban planning, which is a process, in essence both technical and political, that focuses on the progress and design of land use. It also focuses on "the built environment," which includes infrastructure interacting with air and water, and the utilization of transportation, communications, and supply networks. For historical origins, as soon as individuals began joining together in communities, we have the birth of urban planning. Archaeologists have discovered vestiges of urban planning in ancient Mesopotamia, for example, angular fixations made for street ways. The desire to make living together in large groups functional is what drives urban planning. This has continued throughout the centuries. Part and parcel of Walt's EPCOT is urban planning. In fact, a large portion of Sam Gennawey's book *The Promise of Progress City* is devoted not to EPCOT, but to understanding urban planning.

Walt used this interest in city design and urban planning and turned to what he perceived was a paramount issue of the early 1960s: urban blight and suburban distraught. Walt became focused on finding a solution for these problems. He felt new technologies and a creative philosophy could transform generations of future city planners into envisioning what is possible. When Walt looked East, he was not looking at solely creating another Disneyland, he was looking to create the next great American City. A city of progress and pleasure that could be visited and learned from. A living, breathing tool of exceptionalism that would feed into the current of cultural and urban development. He was looking to create a new city that would exhibit the latest technological advances and innovative governance to show how people around the world could live a great big beautiful tomorrow.

Walt was after the grandiose; not cutting corners, but going big in a time when others would shy away. This is a risk, but if you win, you win big. As such, Walt began formulating a business plan, a plan that would always be in state of becoming, open to change as needed. He realized something— the future caught up with futurists quicker than they would like. As such, his Community of Tomorrow would not be a tomorrow set in stone, but a tomorrow always advancing. One that would keep moving forward.

Walt wanted to move away from the automobile that had become a predominant fixture in cities and suburban life. This was also an issue visited by urban planners across the world. For example, in the late 1950s, English architect, urban planner, and landscape designer Sir Geoffrey Jellicoe developed an idea for a "future town" that tackled the automobile issue head on. He named it Motopia. The name was unusual, as it seemed to imply more automobiles, or as the authors over at the World Architecture blog say, "Sounds like a dystopian settlement intended only for cars." The plan was to build a Garden City with a grid work of modern buildings. Parks and waterways would be included in between the buildings. It would be a town for 30,000 residents. The main attribute was the roads would be above your head, connecting the tops of buildings with bridgeways, so cars would not impact the ground level. Additionally, there would be motorized walkways for people to use. The plan was also to utilize the waterways with water buses for additional transportation. There would be a connection to a rail station, as well as such amenities as immense green areas and parks, a yacht club, schools, and churches. As far as the design elements, there would be different architects working on the buildings, and from there Jellicoe predicted they could create "inventive and entertaining" variations. A model was built of the town, but the town itself was never constructed. The collective and political will to build such an innovative city could not be summoned, even a site had been found. An illustrated version of a futuristic Motopia also appeared as one of Arthur Radebaugh's weekly visions of the future, undoubtedly increasing the exposure of Jellicoe's ideal town.

Author T.F. Tierney finds that "visionary cities" were in vogue during the late 1950s and 1960s. Tierney is one of the few sources that I have seen that properly speak of Motopia and Walt's EPCOT jointly. Tierney finds them as part of a movement during this time, affixing them with the label of "visionary cities." The ultimate issue for "visionary cities" always came down to bringing them to life. As Tierney contends, the logistics around governance and contested processes usually ended up grounding these visions. Essentially, people gum up the works. These issues are ones that Walt would grapple with in his set up of EPCOT. The Disney company would seek to avoid contested processes by being the sole party in control and would aim to be that in the governance part as well.

As far as the practical elements of Motopia, architect Tom Turner engaged in a bit of retroventurism. Turner reasoned, if built to specifications, the main issue with Motopia was the automobile traffic was wrongly placed above. Issues such as noise, vibrations, and air pollution would creep into Motopia. Turner noted the correct approach would be to place traffic underground; on this Walt would agree based upon his designs for EPCOT.

Walt wanted to create a place where children, teenagers, young adults, and mature citizens could be fully entertained. Removing the idleness that he thought fostered blight would be key, being replaced by self-enjoyment, purpose, leisure, and technology. Walt needed many things to begin to implement his ideas. While his ideas were in state of flux, early on there was one constant in that plan: Walt needed land, land, and more land. Enough land that would allow him and his team to implement the impossible, to construct reality out of dreams.

One item that limited Walt in his Disneyland designs in California was the aforementioned need for space. Disneyland was placed in an area of urban sprawl. This afforded Disneyland with ample access to visitors and tourists, and Walt could fashion Disneyland to his exact specifications. But once a visitor lifted their gaze beyond the park walls, they could be affronted with a city outside of Walt's control aimed at latching on to Disney's success. Disneyland was effectively landlocked, as purchasing land outside the park would require vast investment as the landowners held all the cards and knew the value. When the searching began in the East, it began with a vision for a large blank canvas. Florida would eventually provide that canvas.

What drove Walt to Central Florida, and specifically south of Orlando, was an array of attractive options, number one being a large amount of essentially empty land. Land big enough to build a city and still have space that would buffer it from the outside world. It was a utopian-esque plan with a mix of practical considerations. While the land Disney purchased was virtually a large swamp, there was room for opportunity. There were recently constructed highways in the vicinity of the area in which Disneyland East would be built, as well as soon-to-be finalized major interchanges. These features would allow easy traffic flow of visitors into the region. The nearby highways are the Florida Turnpike and I-4, which both cut through Florida from North to South (Turnpike) and East to West (I-4) directly near the land Walt would eventually choose. The importance of having the land easily accessible by visitors and guests was a key concern.

Now, Walt was not the first to design a city to be owned by a company with commercial interests at play. Company towns were a known element. A company town is town where all commercial entities, grocer, restaurants, banks, etc. are built and owned by a single company, in addition to all the residences. These tended to crop up in remote areas such as railroad construction or lumber camps. Sometimes they were built as a utopian workers' village, with churches, schools, and other residential-based amenities. However, these towns were open to abuse; without commercial competition, housing costs and food in company towns could become exorbitant. The workers would go in debt; sometimes these company towns were more prison camps than actually cities. Walt was aiming for the utopian-esque version in his EPCOT.

Regardless of Walt's altruistic goals, his city would effectively be a commercial enterprise. It would not be a company town but more a themed urban center. Walt was not the first to desire building a themed city in Florida, though. Despite the grandiose nature of EPCOT, it was, at the end of the day, a city based upon a central underlying theme, that of futuristic American innovation. There is an interesting example of a themed city in Florida prior to Disney's Florida land purchase that we will explore together.

eXperimental Tip: The company town—you can check out any time you want, but you can never leave. Is there a middle ground between prison work camp and utopian company town? What roles should commercial entities and interests have in urban planning? Let us tackle a broad question when it comes to urban planning or effectively planning out a city's core elements: What is the most important element when planning a city? At its basic level, urban planning deals with three main and competing zoning elements: *residential* (people's homes), *commercial* (business locations), *industrial* (production facilities and distribution centers). Some would argue that urban planning should be resident-focused, with commercial and industrial being addressed to answer the residential needs. EPCOT, we will come to see, was a design where commercial interests would be primary with the aim of showcasing residents and industry. How most planning occurs however is the industry takes root, and residents flock for the employment, and then commercial moves in to capitalize on the new residents. Government at times can manipulate this by taking the place of industry—think of the origins of such cities as Washington D.C. or Brasilia where government capitals were placed in theretofore unpopulated areas. What consideration should be first: residential, industrial, or commercial? Should they all be weighed equally or weighed based upon need?

What was the other theme-based commercial city in Florida? If you are familiar with the city of Miami and its adjoining metropoles, you still may not even know about its stylistic, urban, and thematic history. The Miami metropoles of Coral Gables, Hialeah, Miami Springs, and Opa-locka had their origins in enterprising businessmen building in the midst of the great Florida land boom of the 1920s. These were men such as George Merrick, a land developer whose father had purchased wide breadths of land; Glenn Curtiss, a famed aviator and inventor;[6] and James Bright, a cattleman who owned immense tracks of land around the Miami area. Merrick focused his attention on south Miami with Coral Gables whilst Curtiss and Bright linked forces to develop areas to the north, out of what became known as the Bright-Curtiss Ranch.

As far as Coral Gables, researcher Stefania Aimar notes "[t]he historic City of Coral Gables was designed and developed starting from 1921 as a full-fledged new town, following the dreams and vision of its founder George

---

6 Glen Curtiss has been likened to the Steve Jobs and Elon Musk of his time, or more poignantly An All American Badass!

Merrick." Coral Gables was not meant to be merely a suburb of Miami; it was a city that incorporated many of the up and coming urban planning themes, such as Garden City. While not a basic suburb, Coral Gables was resident-focused. For example, Merrick did not seek to incorporate industrial complexes but sought to ensure Coral Gables' connectedness to employment opportunities in Miami proper. There eventually would be the development of educational employment opportunities in Coral Gables. Additionally, it was not a themed city, but a stylized city. Its style was called Mediterranean. As Aimar confirms, "through the study and the fine processing of the examples of the architecture of the Mediterranean coasts, in particular the Spanish, Italian and Moorish architecture, a new American architecture was defined, the Mediterranean Style, which could adapt and integrate better with the subtropical climate typical of the Florida region."[7] So while Coral Gables was a Garden City, it did not so much have a theme as it did a beautiful style. For themed cities, we must search elsewhere.

Glenn Curtiss and James Bright owned approximately 120,000 acres north of Miami. With that land, Curtiss and Bright first developed the city of Hialeah, which was known as the Gateway to the Everglades, or the City of Progress.[8] As such, in a similar story to Walt Disney, Curtiss and Bright did succeed in their first foray into real estate development, but Hialeah had limitations. Hialeah, whose stylistic sense was based upon Spanish architecture, developed too rapidly and was unyielding. It had interesting attributes, as it was a city focused on sport and amusement. Horse racing and golf began to take hold, as well as the Miami Motion Pictures Studios. It was truly a destination town but grew outside of the perfect control that Curtiss and Bright had imagined and took on a mixed match life of its own.

Curtiss and Bright, however, had a second shot with the City of Miami Springs, originally named Country Club Estates. The land allocated for this city was still coming out of the Bright-Curtiss Ranch. From the outset, Bright and Curtiss were focused on a much more resident-focused, stringent zoning structure. This was to avoid the sporadic issues that arose in Hialeah's development. The centralized style for this city was to be pueblo architectural style. While that style was incorporated in parts, it was not what would be considered an overriding theme of the town. Their sales brochures for lots reinforced controlled zoning while also advertising plush leisure activities. In a sense, Miami Springs would be the Curtiss and Bright answer to Merrick's

---

7 This reminds me of the Mid-Atlantic accent, or as it is also known as the Transatlantic accent, which is an accent of English that blends together the fanciest features of American and British English. Versions of this can be seen in the television show *Frazier*. Mediterranean style is not a theme but an amalgamation of the best part of various styles fitted to the Florida environ.
8 No relation to Progress City that I have been able to determine.

Coral Gables. Miami Springs has since flourished as a residential-focused community much as Coral Gables, which has benefited from the arrival of the University of Miami.

The third and final of the cities built on land owned by Curtiss and Bright was the most ambitious and most divisive, Opa-locka. It is a development that would lead to a split between the two landowners. It became apparent to Bright, as well as many others, including even Curtiss, that by the mid-1920s the Florida land boom was ending. But Curtiss, with the help of inspiration from family and friends, sought to build a visionary jewel of a city. Bright would drop out, but Curtiss had the financial capabilities to fight against the downfall that came with the end of the land boom. Curtiss pressed ahead with building a city the likes of which had never been known.

Pressing ahead was something Glenn Curtiss was used to. Besides being considered the father of naval aviation through the development of naval airplanes that would be used by the United States and its allies during WWI, Curtiss was also a thrill seeker. Through his interest in motorcycles and innovative engines, he was at one point known as the Fastest Man on Earth, reaching speeds of almost 140mph in 1907 on a motorcycle of his own design. As for aviation, in 1908 he also won a Scientific American Trophy for the first public flight of at least 1km. His company's planes made up a considerable amount of the naval airplanes used in WWI. In 1919, one of his planes was the first to make the Atlantic Ocean crossing, paving the way for long distance flight. Curtiss was a man ahead of his time and truly a larger-than-life figure. But in Florida he was no longer after just speed and flight; he wanted to build a better way to live.

Left to his own devices, Curtiss was encouraged by his mother to reach out to the dashing urban designer Bernhardt Emil Muller. Following his mother's advice, Curtiss reached out to the Nebraska born, Paris trained, globe-trotting Muller. According to historian and poet Frank S. Fitzgerald-Bush (whose family was one of the first residents of Opa-locka), Muller wanted to design "a medieval English village, at its center a castle with towers and embattlements to serve as the civic administration center; along winding lanes would stand thatched-roof cottages, or small English manor houses of brick and half-timber." Funny enough, a castle in the center of a designed space is something that Walt Disney would later name a "weenie." A "weenie" is a central architectural element that would serve as a visual magnet for visitors, much as Sleeping Beauty's castle does in Disneyland.

Opa-locka[9] was envisioned as something different. Its weenie would be of

9 The earliest names of Opa-locka differed from one-word Opalocka, to two words but capitalized differently, Opa-Locka vs. Opa-locka. I have picked what feels most comfortably to me.

an Arabian palace. The city would be themed after Arabian Nights. Rumor has it a family friend of Curtiss, Irene Bush, made a fleeting comment to Curtiss how Muller's idea of a city rising from the swamp with a castle in the middle sounded like a vision out of Arabian Nights, which thus transfixed Curtiss's vision on those tales. As such, Curtiss decided the theme in his city would be Arabian Nights, and he assured Muller there was enough land to explore further options.[10] So without Bright, Curtiss the Inventor was unleashed. Opa-locka was to be not just a residential community, but a total community with space for industry and business as well.

Curtiss went full aspirational, seeking to bring art to life. As Merrick had done in Coral Gables, Curtiss sought to incorporate the Garden City[11] model and allow for open space and maximum leisure. Curtiss sought to immortalize what a fully self-sufficient American Garden City could be. Opa-locka was specifically zoned, but those zones were for residential, commercial, industry, and leisure. Residents were afforded their own separate garden plots to raise food. The city itself was meant to be self-sufficient and self-contained with an immense number of amenities. These amenities included an airport, zoo, swimming pools, parks, golf course, fairgrounds, archery clubs, and additional garden plots. All of the structures, including its City Hall, train station, residences, and businesses were built in the Arabian Night theme, as designed by Muller. Interestingly, Curtiss had planned to build additional themed areas in Opa-locka—Egyptian, Chinese, and Muller's suggested English. But it was to Arabian Nights Curtiss and Muller turned first, and that infused every early aspect, even down to the street names.

As Glenn himself described it, Opa-locka would be the perfect city of which urban planning and engineering could achieve. It was planned to meet all the needs, physical and mental, of the residents of the city.[12] The uniqueness of Opa-locka was to be expressed in its architecture. The unspecified Mediterranean style that dominated cities such as Coral Gables would not be sufficient. Opa-locka would need more than a style; it would need a theme. A theme is akin to an overall visual look that is developed to bring about an ideal or story, e.g.. Arabian Nights. A style is a well-organized set of components collected purposefully to bring about a certain atmosphere and artistic pattern, e.g.. Mediterranean Style.

Curtiss sought to invite employment opportunities in manufacturing,

10 There are some sources that point to Muller as coming up with the idea for Arabian Nights.
11 *Cough, cough*, we have seen this term before, maybe you should spend some time to research amongst yourselves.
12 The fact we have a reference to mental needs is intriguing, as it represents an early holistic approach to urban planning. This language was pulled from source from writing in the 1970s, so it is unclear whether this was the aim of Curtiss in the 1920s or the aim of Curtiss through the lens of 1970s.

construction, and service to bring the self-sufficiency of Opa-locka to apex. Opa-locka would also have a commuter train service, one of the first in Miami. It really was shaping up to be a city like no other at the time, adopting novel development ideals and a thematic approach. Its Arabian Night thematic overtures were on full display when the rail line was officially opened.

In 1927, upon the first train arrival, Opa-locka's residents and hired actors streamed forth to greet the train. In fact, an entire production and battle scene was played out before the notable visitors, which included the then-Florida governor. With the construction essentially completed of the City Hall, train station, joint police and fire station, golf course, several store fronts and gas stations, apartment complexes, horse stables, residences, elementary school, and even an observation tower in which to view the burgeoning city, the future of Opa-locka looked bright. The city contained one of the first zoos in Florida, featuring local wildlife, and its Arabian Night themed pool put on shows for packed crowds. Curtiss even deployed private Opa-locka buses to bring in tourists from Miami for these shows and the zoo. It was a unique gem in the Florida land boom that embraced an idealized urban planning of self-sufficiency and entertainment. Unfortunately, the best laid plans fell to ruin as triple tragedy struck.

The first was in 1926 with a hurricane that decimated Miami, but Opa-locka was left relatively unscathed. As such, there was hope for continued survival, but then the stock market crash dealt a financial blow that halted growth. Curtiss could not bear the financial burden of keeping the city afloat, as such all new construction was to be postponed. However, the final tragedy hit when shortly thereafter Opa-locka's creator died.

Curtiss dying in 1930 seemed to seal the city's fate and the potential realization of his plans fell to the wayside. There would be no additional themes, and all new construction that was stopped due to the depression was never taken back up. Opa-locka lost its visionary and would never be able to achieve its initial promise. In 1959, Bernhardt Muller returned to the city 30 years after he had last seen it and was affronted with normality, something he would never allow in his design. Many of his unique plans and specifications had been demolished, and standard functional dwellings had assumed their place. He left despondent, affronted with normalcy and hideous colors (at least to him), and the town folk grew angry at him for his critiques on their city. Today, even the crown jewel, the City Hall, which had at once been reinvigorated in the late 1980s after years of disrepair has again fallen on hard times as the City of Opa-locka succumbed to recent internal strife, immense financial waste, crime, and administrative encumbrance. Further restoration of City Hall and or other elements of the town were not completed and continue to sustain deterioration.

> **eXperimental Tip:** The riders who took part in the Arabian Nights themed battle that greeted the arriving train in Opa-locka's earliest days wore brown faces. The city's theme is arguably both an homage but also a form of cultural appropriation. I always wanted to unpack this idea personally, but heretofore have been unable to separate time to do so. Maybe you can take up the mantle. Opa Locka (the name was later morphed) as it now stands is in a precarious position, and its original vision belonged to a time period of the past. Many of the historic buildings and homes in the city do survive and carry on the Arabian Nights motif. While the City Hall lays abandoned and surrounded by chain linked fence, the city has one of the highest, if not highest number of Moorish revival structures in the United States, though many are in need of repair or outright reconstruction. Are any of them are worth saving? Are they vestiges of cultural appropriation or cultural appreciation? If they are cultural appropriation, does that automatically prohibit their restorative value? These are some interesting questions to explore individually or in a class setting.

Even though the dream of Opa-locka failed to survive, its plan was enviable. As one of the few cities that sought to fully emulate the Garden City design, in addition to being self-sufficient, it was a town ahead of its time. The list of amenities was enough to drive an immense early interest, coupled with its amazingly unique theme. It brings out the best of retroventurism, including a daring undertaking, but with the passing of time there was a snap of loss of vision: What could have been?

We can see that for plans of this scale to come to fruition there must be a group vision not just held by one man. There must be a roadmap for future generations and an interest to keep those dreams alive. In 1959, Muller tried to reinvigorate interest in Curtiss's Opa-locka, but too much time had passed, and he was repaid for his imploring when the citizens grabbed their torches and pitchforks. Walt Disney knew this all too well, as he would affirm that one must think beyond their own lifetime to do something truly worthwhile.

We will revisit Opa-locka throughout this book. It should be noted that

Glenn Curtiss had the good fortune to run into James Bright, who had one main item that is needed in developing a city; yep, you know it: land. Walt did not have a James Bright waiting to do business with him, nor was Walt looking for a business partner. But Walt would still need to find the land to achieve his dreams, hence his head being turned to south of Orlando, Florida. This takes us to the next stop on our retroventurism tour, the Great Florida Land Purchase.

CHAPTER 3
Living in the Land of Contracts

Swamps, secrets, and savings: these were at the heart of Walt Disney's Florida land deal. In order to get the amount of land he wanted, it would need to be cheap and unused. Florida had a lot of that, but it was mostly swamp land. For the land to remain cheap, no one could know that Walt Disney was the one looking to buy up all that swamp land. So, to ensure the land remained cheap, he needed to keep his identity (and his company's identity) secret as he entered into agreements to secure all that land.

When Walt first decided to lock up the land he desired south of Orlando, Florida, he used a special kind of contract called an option contract. These option contracts allowed Walt to gain effective control of his land dealings without fully committing himself until the time was right. All of this was done under the cover of secrecy. If word got out that Disney was buying land in Florida, or even thinking of it, the price of the land would skyrocket. Walt did not want to overpay for the land he desired. These option contracts provide us a great opportunity to learn about contracts and their relationship with business law.

Contracts are the current that churns in the midst of the business law river. Contracts are, at the end of day, agreements or promises between two or more parties (not the happy birthday kind of party but another name for an individual or entity involved in an agreement), which are enforceable by the government. The enforceable part is key, and what really makes contracts a perfect example of business and law. Without enforceability, contracts would be utterly worthless and void of purpose. They would simply represent the intent of the parties without a mechanism to ensure their fulfillment.

Contracts in general are also, well, a generally interesting concept. Why do we need to enforce promises? Should not people know better than to trust other people? Although it may seem counterintuitive, the enforcement of contracts encourages trust. The old, I *better get that in writing because I do not trust you* adage is an interesting one. Why would getting it in writing change the nature of trust? Well, contracts encourage trust based upon reliance of enforceability; you are, in fact, becoming more trustful of them to complete the promise because you can force them to if they fail. The person or the promise does not change with a contract; the world around the person and the promise do.

I know this is a circular argument, but I hope you follow because it is a neat one. You enter into a contract for the exchange of future products, but payment from you is required now, and you do so with the added belief that the contract will be enforced if need be. Without a contract, you would presumably be unwilling to take such risks because of the lack of trust of it being completed. The reason being mainly because you have no means to enforce it (well, besides, you know, going and taking what is owed to you). A society without contracts is a less trusting one, as an enforceable contract allows you to trust a promise made. I know, it is circular.

But where do contracts come from? The key again is checking enforceability. As far as western legal systems go, you get the foundations of contract law in Greek and Roman culture. You can turn to Justinian's Code, the Roman (or Byzantine) code of laws from the 6th century CE. Justinian's Code codifies what was already a developed understanding of contracts. The most important being enforcement of promises to be carried out after they were made. It may not seem like a novel concept, but it took some time to get there. In Europe during the period between Roman control and the rise of the Medieval era (aka the Dark Ages), enforceability was the main lacking factor in keeping contract law alive. It was not until the rise of medieval guilds and mercantile courts[13] that we again see the ability to enforce promises of future events begin to take hold. It was from those medieval mercantile courts that contract law was born anew and eventually cemented into the judiciary of medieval and Renaissance Europe.

> eXperimental Tip: The Rise and Fall of the Fabled Lex Mercatoria! What was it? Why was it? Who was it? Lex Mercatoria, or in modern English, Mercantile Law, is a form of law in which merchants pass judgment on fellow merchants without the use of formal government courts. There are some interesting forms of self-regulating professions still in existence, much like a medieval guild. The first that comes to mind is one of which I am member: a state bar association for lawyers. In some states, the ability to remove a lawyer from the practice of law does not reside with administrative courts (i.e. an extension of the governor), but from their state bar association itself (some given this power

---

13 The mercantile courts were medieval courts run by merchants for merchants. There is strong debate, however, as to their unchecked authority, i.e. did their respective crown and/or local bishop control them or did they truly exercise unilateral power? Stephen E. Sachs's law review article, *From St. Ives to Cyberspace* makes for an interesting read if you want to learn more.

through their state court system). In fields such as international trade and cyberspace, questions abound as to whether Lex Mercatoria should make a comeback. The question is whether it is best for local domestic courts to deal with such large global fields, or should disputes arising in these global fields be decided by independent third parties familiar with the area? Third parties that can render decisions based on custom or maybe even their own developed internal regulations. It is a fair enough question as to whether a business or a profession should regulate itself given that they are best situated to understand the issue. But the counter of that is we have a functioning judicial system in most countries and removal of control over disputes from those judicial systems is an affront to their sovereign authority, as such cases should remain in domestic courts. What do you think? For some extra guidance, check out the articles mentioned in the previous footnote by Stephen Sachs.

Now that we know a little bit about where contracts came from, and some circular conversations about trust are behind us, I can tell you how a standard contract works and then go into a little more detail about option contracts. Again, the main push behind contracts is enforceability. Without it, you have an empty promise worth the handshake it was given with or the paper it was scratched out on. Now, courts overtime determined, and eventually governments codified, what a contract needs in order to be enforceable. The needs are broken down into what we call the elements of contract. The basic four elements are: (1) *offer*; (2) *acceptance*; (3) *consideration*; and (4) *legality*.

Offer and acceptance are the easiest to tackle; an offer must be made by one party and the second party must accept it. This is the agreement portion of a contract. There are some fun items that you can play around with when working to understand offer and acceptance by learning about counteroffers and revocation. A counteroffer will negate an original offer and thus becomes the new offer, which the first party will either accept or reject. Also, an acceptance must be communicated, so none of the "if you accept this offer do not say anything" tricks can be pulled. As far as revocation, a frequent example of how one can revoke an offer or acceptance is usually displayed by the use of mailed offers. A revocation is a cancelling of either the offer or the sale. For example, Party 1 mails an offer to buy a car for $3,000.00, and that offer is received by Party 2 three days later (Day 3). Party 2 takes two days to mail her acceptance (Day 5), and Party 1 receives that response three days later (Day 8). Party one can only revoke his offer up until Day 5, which is the time when Party 2 actually sat down to communicate acceptance. Further, Party 2 can revoke that acceptance up until Day 8, which is the time that Party 1 actually receives the acceptance mailed. Things can always become more complex with offer and acceptance, but at its base level it is how parties reach an agreement.

Consideration is an important contract element as well. It is essentially the items that are bargained for and received in the contract. It must be present for both parties. Consideration in most contracts can be found if there is a price mentioned and a good sold. I will sell you this fancy hat for one penny. The hat and the one penny are the consideration. Now, consideration does not have to be a dollar amount; it can be something of value in exchange for an agreement to do something or even not to do something. Consideration is what draws the person into the agreement, a process that is legally termed as inducing them to enter into a contract. This is also what separates a contract from a promise of a gift. A promised future gift is not an enforceable contract, as it lacks consideration on one side.

The last one is probably the most fun to work out in a classroom setting and is the most connected to law; that is legality. Legality refers to a court's decision not to enforce illegal or unconscionable contracts. A contract for example to buy cocaine (if cocaine has somehow become legal in the future, then simply insert another illegal drug. If there are no illegal drugs then wow, the future sounds out there) is unenforceable because cocaine is illegal and a court will not allow it. This is similar to how contracts should not be enforced against minors or individuals with a reduced mental capacity, whether by age, mental health, or mental impairment. But legality also starts the void and voidable debate, which is fun to work through as well. A void contract is one that never existed; it's void for a reason as prescribed by law. A voidable contract is one that does exist but can be declared void if the party against whom it is held wants to void it. For example, a drunk person signs a great deal on new car, but when he sobers up and sees the signed contract, it turns out he wants the car even though he does not remember signing the contract. That contract to buy the car is voidable, not void, as our partying friend can choose to go through with the contract, forcing the dealership to sell the car. An additional element of legality in some states is that certain contracts must be in writing; for example contracts to buy land in Florida must be in writing. You cannot have a handshake deal on a real estate contract.

This gives you the basic ins and outs of contracts. You can use these basics like points of interest on a map; you are always free to visit and explore these areas in much greater detail on your own. Speaking of exploringspecifics, let's explore some with the option contract.

The option contract is a fun contract tool. It lives under the buy and sell contract umbrella, meaning it deals with something that is offered for sale and another person wants to buy it. Option contracts actually have a lot to do with the first element of contracts we discussed above, which is offers. Option contracts can appear in real estate dealings, and it is real estate we will focus on.

Let me give you an example. A ranch owner wants to sell her land, so she puts a for-sale sign on her property for $10,000.00. A young businessman comes by, sees a great opportunity to develop a movie theater on that land, and wants to buy it. The businessman still needs more land, so he wants to know if he can also buy land nearby the ranch first before he commits to buying the ranch. He sees some other people looking at the for-sale sign and is worried someone might swoop in on the ranch deal. He approaches the ranch owner and offers her $500.00 if the ranch owner agrees not to sell the land for 30 days. In addition, the ranch owner is to sell the land to the businessman within those 30 days for the price listed if the businessman decides he wants it. The ranch owner agrees, and an option contract has been entered into between our young savvy businessman and the ranch owner looking to make a valuable sale. That is an option contract.

What are some things an option contract is not? An option contract is not a counteroffer. It is a new contract where the potential land buyer becomes the one making an offer to the landowner to not do something (i.e. sell the land to someone else for a period of time and not raise the price). Additionally, it is not acceptance of the offer to buy the land. If during the option period the potential buyer decides it is not worth it, the buyer is not required to buy the land. Nor does that mean the price listed will be the price finally agreed to, during the option period (or even after) the price is subject to change. If the land has not been sold, the potential buyer can counter-offer at a lower price, and the seller could agree. It is a nifty tool and one that Walt Disney used excellently during his Florida land purchase.

Walt's road to the option contracts is an interesting one. The Disney company began making specific inquiries into the land south of Orlando as early as November 1963. A young Disney associate by the name of Bill Lund paid a visit to a real estate broker David Nusbickel, of Florida Ranch Lands during this time. Lund gave no indication he was a Disney associate and paraded about as if he was simply searching for a lot of land for a large investor. In fact, Lund was specifically instructed by Disney to keep his relationship secret. Walt was fearful of skyrocketing land prices if even a peep got out that Disney was looking for new land. It was a valid concern. As such, Lund remained vague and Nusbickel was none the wiser. In fact, Lund had been outfitted with a business card and cover at a law firm called Burke & Burke in New York. Burke & Burke, an actual law firm, was located one floor below the Disney company's outside legal counsel William Donovan's office. As we will learn in a moment, Donovan was no stranger to secrecy.

Proceeding in their conversations, Nusbickel gave a real estate brochure to Lund, featuring a sizable tract of land commonly called the Demtree Tract. Nusbickel also referenced two other adjacent tracts, the Bay Lake Tract and the Hamrick Tract. Lund thanked Nusbickel and went on his way. It is alleged that Nusbickel informed Lund that the Florida Ranch Lands would ask for a ten percent commission on any real estate deal for these three tracts of land. Nusbickel tried following up with Lund through Burke & Burke, but conversations eventually fizzled out. Lund had returned to California with the brochure and information.

There is some back and forth as to when the exact moment was that the Disney company finally decided on buying land south of Orlando. Once Lund returned with the brochure and information gained, it was passed on to Walt and the central Disney team. After a series of meetings between Walt and his team, it was decided that Central Florida would indeed be the location, and they needed someone to lock in the property. Bob Foster, in-house counsel for the Disney Company, was put in charge to make it so.

Foster would travel to Florida under the name of Bob Price in order keep his identity secret, as he was a sufficiently known person and would be easily found in Disney employment rolls. Foster reached out to William Donovan for help in locating a Florida attorney. Disney wanted someone with a similar skill in secrecy who could help get their needed land deals over the line. Donovan, as it turns out, had been in the U.S. military, specifically the Office of Strategic Services (precursor to the CIA). According to some, William Donovan's nickname was "Wild Bill," but more intriguing, he is also known as the "Father of the CIA."[14] Donovan's firm also a featured a future director of the CIA as one of the firm's founding members.

Needless to say, Donovan was good at the kind of work Disney needed during this time. But Foster wanted someone local in Florida. As such, Wild Bill reached out to a man he knew he could trust, a former member of the same Strategic Services department, Paul Helliwell. Helliwell added Roy

---

14 In fact, the CIA has a nice write up about William Donovan and his work with the CIA, even included in its Kid's Zone portion of the website.

Hawkins, a gifted real estate consultant, to the mix. Everyone was made aware of the secrecy and the scope of land needed.

Disney wanted between 7,000 and 12,000 acres in Florida. To give a quick insight into scope, Disneyland in California when it first opened was sitting on only 160 acres. To get that much land, Disney needed to ensure secrecy each step of the way. If word got out, land value would rise across the state. As such, Foster, Helliwell, and Hawkins used every trick in the book to keep Walt's plan under wraps.

For example, calls between Helliwell's office in Miami and Disney were directed through Donovan's New York office, and the messages were relayed to California. Undoubtedly, if it was a matter of urgency, Disney team members could be reached in California and respond in real time to the staff at the New York office. Additionally, Hawkins, while he was property hunting in Florida for Disney, would travel to other cities such as Seattle and send postcards to random acquaintances in and around Central Florida. Seattle being the headquarters of Boeing, a company who could be charged with looking for land on the scale Disney was. As such, some rumors began to swell that it was actually Boeing looking for land in the area. Utilizing all this secrecy and searching through the Spring of 1964, including looking into other potential areas in Central Florida, it was finally decided that the tracts Lund had brought back would make for the best location, in addition to others nearby.

Hawkins initiated all the deals, some with the assistance of the same Florida Ranch Lands real estate office. Florida Ranch Lands was not treated as the initiating agent, Hawkins was. As such, it resulted in split commissions on the eventual real estate deals. Starting in May 1964 and continuing through the summer, option contracts were entered into for Demtree Tract, the Bay Lake Tract, the Hamrick Tract. All options were done using Helliwell's name, with no connection to Disney. However, there was still a host of issues that needed be cleared. There were historical subdivisions to be cleaned up and cleared out. Subsurface soil rights that had been sold off by the landowners needed to be regained, and some reluctant smaller lot owners who would not easily budge.[15] Walt and his team were able to get past each hurdle.

Disney utilized option contracts to secure more land than they originally intended, and they were not done yet. The three tracts discussed were all located in Orange County, but Disney saw an opportunity to expand their reach with some available land in neighboring Osceola County. To secure the

15 A couple owned some pleasant acreage right on Bay Lake (their little piece of heaven) and were not eager to give it up. Disney's team had to ask local government officials to step in to smooth things over, which they eventually did.

Osceola land, commonly known as the Bronson parcel, after the state senator Irlo Bronson who owned it, Disney would not be using an option contract. Walt wanted to purchase the land outright. He still needed to do so in secret, and any land purchase agreement would become public record. So how could Walt buy the land and still keep the Disney company from the spotlight? To answer that question, we turn to our next chapter, The Many Business Entities of Walt Disney.

CHAPTER 4
The Many Business Entities of the Talented Mr. Disney

In the mid-1960s, a thereto unknown international investment team, a highway expansion corporation, and a ranching company were all separately buying large swaths of swamp land in the middle of Florida. Unbeknownst to almost all, however, was that those companies were not at all what they seemed. Indeed, they were all just recently incorporated for one purpose and owned by a single entity. An entity that was a domestic entertainment conglomerate bent on secrecy. Welcome to the Many Business Entities of the Talented Mr. Disney.

In an earlier chapter, I discussed the historical rise of business entities. Business entities play a pivotal role in business law education, and the topics related solely to those entities are often taught in separate courses in law schools and business programs. Business entities also afford an amazing segue into discussing the next phase of Walt Disney's Florida land purchase. The setting up of several "secret" companies in order to execute the final deals to buy the land Disney needed. But before we continue on to the cloak and dagger stuff, let us take a look at what types of modern-day business entities exist.

One thing to be upfront about is that business entities, while generally the same throughout the United States because of Federal tax laws, can be treated quite differently when you go from state to state. That is not even taking in to account some of the many different types of business entities in other countries that mirror American ones in some shade or form. I will touch on as much as I can to give you the basics.

One of the easiest locations to learn the general basics of the various types of American business entities—well, besides this book, of course (shameless plug in case you happen to randomly open to this page prior to buying; if not, well, you bought it already so...)—is IRS.gov. The Internal Revenue Service lists five basic types of business entities:(1) *Sole proprietorships*, (2) *Partnerships*, (3) *Corporations*; (4) *S corporations*; and (5) *Limited liability companies*. I will touch on each in turn while providing historical background when necessary.

The sole proprietorship is perhaps the simplest and most prevalent of the five basic business entities. It consists of you and a business. Yep, that's it. Okay, now on to the next one. I'm kidding; a little bit more background is in order. A sole proprietorship means the business is owned by one person. The business, in essence, is an extension of that person. A sole proprietorship is an unincorporated entity. That means there is no need to file incorporation paperwork with a particular state to begin operating a sole proprietorship. Yet a sole proprietor is usually required to get business licenses and permits in order to lawfully operate. As to being a sole proprietorship, the good news is all the money goes to the owner; bad news is so does all the debt and liabilities. Liabilities can be things such as being sued for running over a person's foot with a bike on a newspaper route. Liabilities are potentially negative issues that can cost the owner personally. An example is that owner's personal assets (car, personal bank savings) could be up for grabs if the person who got their foot run over sues the business for damages and medical expenses. As for putting the business out there, some sole proprietors operate under a fictitious name, sometimes called a d.b.a. (doing business as) name. While this is not incorporating, the owner files paperwork with the state so people can formally recognize the fictitious trade name.

Partnerships are essentially the convergence of two or more sole proprietors. When two or more people decide to enter a business together and split the profits, they may form a partnership. I say may, as there are similar contractual formations out there, like a joint venture. A joint venture is when two or more people or entities come together, but for a specific purpose and maintain separate identities. In a partnership, two or many become the one for the business operation. Partnerships need not be incorporated either, though like sole proprietors, licenses and permits are usually required. In addition, proper tax filing is required as well. The profits, much like sole proprietors, go straight to the partners in the partnership but so do the debts and liabilities. Partnerships can also be subdivided into general partnerships, limited partnerships, limited liability partnership, and, the funniest of all to say, a limited liability limited partnership. Each of these distinctions are settled in partnership agreements between the partners and cover items such as management of the entity and liabilities if things go wrong. Each are nuanced, and not all four types are offered in every state.

Some famous partnerships can be found in everyday products. Proctor & Gamble, P&G for short, maker of many of our most common household goods and products, was a partnership started in 1837 by William Procter and James Gamble. Each were married to a different sister and their father-in-law suggested the two men link up in business; the rest, they say, is history. Another famous partnership can be found in the freezer section of your local super market, Ben & Jerry's ice cream, started by Ben Cohen and Jerry Greenfield. The two friends linked together after neither could find a satisfying job elsewhere and decided to study ice cream making. Ah, a world without Chunky Monkey ice cream would be a darker world indeed.

A corporation is a whole different ball game of sorts. A corporation is considered a separate legal entity from its owners (called shareholders, who own stock in the corporation). A corporation can have one or many shareholders. A corporation's formal name usually must contain the word company, corporation, or incorporated, and their derivations (Co., Corp., Inc.). An example of how a company differs from our entities above is that if a shareholder dies, the corporation does not automatically dissolve like a partnership may. This is because the corporation is a separate entity in and of itself. Like its name, a corporation is incorporated with the state. Incorporation is achieved by filing the aptly named Articles of Incorporation. At the corporation's most basic level tax status, income the company earns usually gets taxed twice: once when the company earns it and again when profits are issued to its owners (this can be adjusted, as we will see next). Corporations require adherence to corporate governance activities and formalities, things such as holding regular shareholder or management meetings. One of the most attractive options for choosing a corporation is the limitation of liability.

Shareholders are normally only liable for the money they actually invest in the company. This money is grouped into what is called the company's assets. Assets can also be other items, such as a building or the toilet paper that it buys for its bathrooms in that building. As you can see, not all assets are equal. The idea, though, is that the only assets at risk are the assets of the company as opposed to the personal wealth of the owners. This then affords risk taking, as there is less to lose. A quick example: if a Your, Inc. employee runs over the foot of someone and Your, Inc. is sued, the unfortunate bystander who keeps getting her foot runover sues against the assets of Your, Inc. not of the owners individually. This is different if it happens as we saw with a sole proprietor; in that instance, the wounded party could go after the personal assets of the owner, not just business assets. If you know your personal assets are protected, you are more willing to take risks, which may pay off immensely.

S corporations (the S stands for Subchapter S of the IRS code), are corporations that are taxed differently. The IRS allows some corporations to elect to be taxed in a special way. The importance here is that income earned by the corporation will only be taxed once at the shareholder level. Income and losses are passed-through to the shareholders, similarly to a partnership, thus eliminating what is often call the corporate double-taxation issue. S corporations must still adhere to other requirements and formalities of corporations in general.

The final commonly recognized business entity is the limited liability company (LLC). The LLC has become quite fashionable in the business realm as the go-to business entity of choice for many small businesses. One main reason is the benefit of pass-through taxation it is generally afforded and the protections of limited liability it offers. The LLC's formal name must indicate its LLC status and thus have "LLC" or "limited liability company" in the name. Unlike an S Corporation, there are less hurdles and size restrictions to becoming an LLC, and there are less corporate governance formalities as well. Transfer of ownership becomes a little trickier with an LLC. The owners, called members, have a much closer and personal tie to their "membership interests" than shareholders do with stocks. Thus there are extra items involved in transfer, but those can be contracted out by using a well-crafted Articles of Organization.

There are a host of other business entities that are separate or fall under these five entity types such as: professional limited liability companies (PLLC), professional associations (P.A.), cooperatives (co-ops), non-for-profits, and non-governmental organizations. There are also different business forms in other countries; a common one is the Private Limited Company (Ltd.) from the United Kingdom. The Ltd. has some similarities to the American LLC in regards to the protections it affords and its overall nature. Differences lie in the standard set up with Ltd. having shareholders and stocks and tax treatment generally, whereby the Ltd. is double taxed. But as far as liability protection, they are modeled in a similar way to protect the owners, as well as their ease of operating as opposed to their more formal counterparts in their respective countries.

This gives us at least a basic working knowledge of business entities and some background on their usefulness. Walt used an assortment of business entities to convert the option contracts into hard firm real estate land contracts. He still wanted to maintain an air of secrecy to avoid any unnecessary price jumps as he moved to close the deals. As such, he tried to pick inauspicious names and remove any traces back to California or the Disney company.

In all, Walt had six corporations set up in and around the fall and winter of 1964, and continuing into 1965. He had five in Florida and one in Delaware. As far as I have been able to determine, they were all formal corporations (in fact, the LLC was not invented until the late 1970s). The five Florida entities were: Tomahawk Properties Inc, Reedy Creek Ranch Inc, AyeFour Corporation,[16] Latin American Development and Management

16 Interestingly, it's actually spelled AyeFour Corpoation with the second "r" missing when I checked the records of Florida's Division of Corporations.

Corporation, and Bay Lake Properties, Inc. It appears the names were created as a further step in confusing those interested in knowing who was purchasing the land. Latin American Development and Management Corporation has the tone of foreign investors, AyeFour seemed to reference the I-4 highway system, and Reedy Creek Ranch has a cattle element to it. These corporations' shares were all eventually owned by a Delaware Company called Compass East Corporation.

I did some digging to see what I could find out about these corporations. Three of the five Florida companies still have information available online through the Florida Division of Corporations—AyeFour, Tomahawk, and Reedy Creedy Ranch. The corporate registration for Tomahawk was filed on October 13, 1964; AyeFour on November 3, 1964; and Reedy Creek Ranch on November 12, 1964. Compass East was filed for on December 9, 1964 in Delaware. AyeFour is the most illuminating of all, as it is the only record of the Florida five that contains easily accessible information. More importantly, the information it does contain matches the air of secrecy around the entire Florida land purchase and Paul Helliwell, the local Miami attorney recommended by Wild Bill Donovan.

Before going into the air of secrecy, the availability of the AyeFour filing also shows Disney had to go through the regular steps in setting up a corporation. A corporation is required to maintain both a physical address and a mailing address. They, of course, can be the same, as was the case with AyeFour. The address listed shows that AyeFour was headquartered with its principal place of business right in the middle of downtown Miami.

Corporations must also appoint a registered agent, which is a party designated by a business to receive legal documents. The registered agent must maintain sufficient business office hours in order to receive said documents, and they must have a Florida address. AyeFour's registered agent was an attorney by the name of Halleck A. Butts. Paul Helliwell and Halleck A. Butts both served as honorary consuls to Thailand, as such my general belief would be that Helliwell knew and appointed Butts to be the registered agent. I have seen their names appear on other legal documentation but cannot state with certainty that they worked at the same firm.

Even more interesting is AyeFour had a full allotment of corporate officers. Included on the Florida Division of Corporations' registration for AyeFour is the listing of the following officers: a President, a Vice President/ Treasurer, and two Secretaries (unusual to have two, but one appears to also be a director as well—directors are also another corporate requirement). These officers and directors are F. Eugene Poe (President and a Director), W.H. Losner (Vice President, Treasurer, and a Director), Vada Martin

(Secretary and a Director), M.J. Melrose (Secretary). All officers share a similar address of a P.O. Drawer in Perrine, Florida. Perrine being a township located near Miami. Out of all of these individuals, I was able to acquire more information about F. Eugene Poe (the "F" stands for Francis, and he also went by the nickname Gene) and M.J. Melrose (the M.J. stands for Mary Jane).

Poe was the President of two South Florida banks, one of those being located in Perrine (maybe the location of the P.O. Drawer). Can you guess who was the boss of both of those banks? At least as far as the late 1960s, it was Paul Helliwell. Melrose, an attorney, was a partner at a prestigious Miami law firm—yep, you guessed it, Helliwell's firm. It seems Helliwell got his friends and colleagues to join the great Disney secret. Now it is unclear if Butts, Melrose, or Poe knew they were part of a secret Disney land grab, but it is still fun to learn about. However, what was happening in the background of Helliwell and his friends' world was just as intriguing.

Allegedly, Helliwell was still operating for the government, specifically the CIA, during this time. Things such as his honorary consul role for Thailand were purportedly not happenstance.[17] He appears to have been a high-ranking national security officer for the United States, focusing on Asian affairs during and after World War II. As author and reporter T.D. Allman finds, Helliwell was relocated to Miami in order to provide business cover for the CIA's Cuba operations. Helliwell was in so deep with the CIA, running operations in the Caribbean, that his activities were apparently unbeknownst to the IRS. The IRS would eventually investigate strange and possibly illicit drug funds that were coming into Poe's banks. The CIA apparently requested the IRS to halt further investigations, presumably in fear of either compromising CIA operations or discovering unsavory connections therein.

Professor Alan A. Block's book *Masters of Paradise* goes into great detail about Paul Helliwell, and it is interesting to see these same names being discussed. It should be noted, Block does not fair on the side that Helliwell's extra-curricular activities (those outside his role as your friendly neighborhood outstanding Florida real estate attorney) were done solely for the purposes of assisting the CIA. There are strong allegations in *Masters of Paradise* that Helliwell was a co-conspirator in tax scams, among many other criminal activities. None of this is laid bare in any connection to Walt or the Disney company, though some of the nefarious activities are alleged to have occurred on the tail end of Helliwell's representation of Disney. In light of that, Block does make a bare bones mention of land deals by Helliwell around Orlando subsequent to Disney's Florida land purchase. In *Masters*

---

17 It is unclear if the same is true of Halleck Butts.

of Paradise, Helliwell is accused of using his banks in Florida as a funneling device for Bahamian and Cayman tax shelters, and then from there numerous illicit speculation and financial activities.

Additionally, it is unclear whether Poe or Melrose had connections with the CIA or the nefarious activities, if true. Melrose, Block claims, was working on payoffs to Prime Minister Pindling during and after the Bahamian move toward independence. It is unclear whether there was a relationship between these payoffs and Helliwell's potentially nefarious aims or his role with the CIA. Poe is also an interesting character, as he supplied direct information to the IRS during its investigation of Helliwell. He did so unwittingly and under false pretenses from an IRS agent. The information provided allowed the IRS to build a case, though they never prosecuted against Helliwell. Interestingly, when government sources indirectly informed Poe of the true aim of the IRS agent in ferreting out tax scams and fraud, as opposed to hunting down drug money, Poe let slip the may have a connection with the CIA. Block does not pay this much mind, nor the news reports that the IRS investigation was called off by the CIA.

I flesh out this topic for an interesting reason, as no Disney-focused source books I have come across mention these details about the individuals listed in AyeFour or go in great detail about Helliwell's CIA connection, even though all mention him quite frequently. It is usually a passing note if they do so. Conversely, Block makes no mention that one of Helliwell's most famous clients (besides the national security of the United States) was the Disney company, even in passing. It should be noted, Helliwell was never fully charged with any illicit activity. The reality may be that what makes a person a great CIA agent also makes that person exceptionally gifted at being a real estate, financial, and land use attorney (especially when secrecy is required).

Interestingly, Helliwell's association with the CIA may have been a known unknown.[18] Whether the same was true for any of Helliwell's colleagues—Melrose, Poe, or Butts[19]—I cannot say. Marvin Davis, a central Disney team

18 This term comes from an answer former Secretary of State Donald Rumsfeld gave concerning knowledge of weapons of mass destruction in Iraq: "Reports that say that something hasn't happened are always interesting to me, because as we know, there are known knowns; there are things we know we know. We also know there are known unknowns; that is to say we know there are some things we do not know. But there are also unknown unknowns—the ones we don't know we don't know. And if one looks throughout the history of our country and other free countries, it is the latter category that tend to be the difficult ones."

19 An interesting side note, I found in one random source a Trade Commissioner named Halleck A. Butts working in Tokyo around 1922. This Halleck A. Butts helped arrange for U.S. Trademark protections in Japan. I note this because our Halleck A. Butts also had the connection to Asia generally in his role Honorary Consul for Thailand. Our Halleck A. Butts graduated law school from the University of Miami in 1962 (according to the Florida Bar) or University of Massachusetts

member during the Florida Project and EPCOT business plan, said this about all the secrecy, "it was really classified stuff. It was CIA." It appears that statement was in jest, but there is always a kernel of truth in every good joke.

Back to the brass tacks. The use of the option contracts, through Helliwell, and the eventual land purchase agreements utilizing the many entities of Walt Disney allowed the Disney company to purchase more land than they had initially deemed required. All told, Disney conducted close to 50 transactions to secure the land. By June of 1965, Disney had effectively gained interest in approximately 27,000 acres, more than double what they had deemed to be at the top of their range. The final price tag was a wedge over $5,000,000.00, or around the tune of less than $200 per acre on average.[20] Walt achieved the unimaginable, purchasing more land than he could dream of at a price that dreams were made of.

The establishment of these various business entities created by the Disney company had served their purpose. All the Florida entities would eventually be merged into the Delaware entity. But as we can see, at least with the AyeFour entity, Disney had to go through all the regular elements of establishing a corporation. They had to appoint a registered agent, directors, and officers, for example. Helliwell was nothing if not diligent in his service of Walt's interests.

This is not the first occasion a potential land buyer sought to shield their identity in order to secure favorable pricing. Although, it does raise some interesting questions in regard to whether the buyer and seller actually had a meeting of the minds. Maybe the seller would not want to sell to Disney because they despised cartoons. One may never know, and the buyers were never afforded that option. Being on the same footing is part and parcel of reaching a fair deal, but we are in business, and no laws were apparently broken based on the use of these shadow companies. But it does raise some ethical questions and we will address in a later chapter.

With the use of the shadow entities, Walt had been able to keep his hand hidden. Yet word was not that far from getting out. The clues were being pieced together by journalists from around the Orlando area. Public officials eventually became in the know, limited though they may have been, and there was concern that Disney would be unable to squash reports. Time was rapidly approaching for Walt to pull back the curtain and make his grand

Lowell (according to the law website Martindale). On this, it appears Miami wins out, as his name appears in alumni magazines. As to our two Hallecks, there is no apparent relationship between the two, but a fun mysterious note nonetheless.

20 Shortly after Disney's name was made public as the land purchaser, prices shot up to about $1,000.00 per acre on the small remaining parcels Disney had been unable to lock up. Additionally, I have seen source note prices that shot up to $75,000.00 per acre on certain areas near the Disney land purchase.

entrance. What was needed now was a public relations campaign like the world had never seen, and in fact may never see again. The Disney company had the perfect person for such a public relations job: the man himself, Walt Disney.

Chapter 5
Relating to the Public Was Never a Problem

Public relations by itself is not a normally recognized chapter in most business law textbooks. The elements that make up public relations law, however, are. I advocate that public relations should be a more recognized field in the area of business law; thus, public relations are a separate chapter in my book. Public relations, in general, focus on the multiple methods a business uses to broadcast messages about its products, services, or overall image. This broadcast is meant to be transmitted to its stakeholders. This is even more important now than during the time of Walt Disney, as there are so many more means to reach the public with the advent of social media and the internet. The platforms for public relations, the laws surrounding them, and the impact upon stakeholders are changing rapidly. Business law textbooks should change with them.

This chapter also brings up one of my favorite subtopics in my business law classes to cover, which is stakeholders. Why, you might ask? Yes, I am asking for you; I hope you do not mind. Stakeholders refer to anyone with an interest, active or potential, in a business's operations. Which turns out, if you think big enough (which you always should), means everyone. Now, there is a close set of stakeholders, people who have a direct or active interest in a business. This close set can include owners, business partners, and employees. If we move further away, we start to meet other stakeholders, such as customers, suppliers, and vendors. Further out we run into the more large-scale stakeholders. These large-scale stakeholders can include communities, governments, the world, future generations, aliens... This list could go on and should go on. Stakeholders refers to people who could have an interest in or could be impacted by the decisions a business makes, and that is what public relations law concerns.

> eXperimental Tip: Are the lyrics, "You can't please everyone, so you've got to please yourself" the best path forward when dealing with stakeholders? Who are the most important stakeholders for a business? Is the customer always right? Shouldn't owners be allowed to keep extra profits, or should the profits be funneled back to the employees? The reality is stakeholder satisfaction is a balancing

act; you simply cannot please everyone all the time. The owners want more money and so do the employees. Well, to achieve that, the business will have to raise prices for customers. If the customers want a cheaper product, the company may need to cut corners on the environmental protections it uses. Who is the most important stakeholder and how can you satisfy one and not hurt the other? These questions also open up a secondary level of inquiry, such as, does a business need to care about the environment or its employees, or need it only to appear to care about them? This is a great place to inject some Machiavelli into business law. According to one of Machiavelli's lines of reasoning, if you are an immoral prince, you must appear to be moral. Machiavelli would contend a company's attempt to appear environmentally friendly to the public even if it internally was not, could be validated as long as it didn't get caught in the deception. What do you think? If no one ever finds out the company is lying and they are saving money and paying their employees more, is that a bad thing? In fact, there are a multitude of business elements you can explore with Machiavelli's *The Prince* by replacing "prince" with "company" or "business owner." Give it a try and see what you discover.

In today's age, the push to convince the public of the favorable pursuits of a company is done through many methods. Public intertest campaigns achieved through social media marketing, metadata exploitation, television advertisements, press conferences, webpages, news releases, speaking engagements, seminars, and community service programs are just some of those ways. Public relations touches so many aspects of both a company's operations and the public eye.

In addition to being so present in today's society, the public relations field is one of the few areas of business law that explicitly interacts with the U.S. Bill of Rights. That connection is through the First Amendment, freedom of speech. After all, what is public relations but speech. U.S. Courts have extended the right to freedom of speech to not only persons, but corporations as well. When a company introduces itself or puts together a promotional ad campaign, these activities can fall under the protection of the First Amendment's freedom of speech provision.

As far as speech, the U.S. Supreme Court has determined there are some restrictions on what constitutes free speech. To break this down, for example, one cannot falsely shout fire in a crowded theatre. That language would not be considered free speech, and thus opens up our shouter to being sued for the damages caused by the panic. The shouter cannot then say, "Well, I have freedom of speech—you can't sue me." The Bill of Rights will not protect that kind of language. In the business realm, a similar unprotected bit of language is fraud in certain contexts.

The right of the federal government, as determined by the Supreme Court, to outline these restrictions against companies' free speech draws from the federal government's ability to regulate interstate commerce as set forth in Section 8 of Article I of the U.S. Constitution (commonly referred to as the Commerce Clause). The ability to place these restrictions on free speech usually does not cover a company's press releases, however they do readily apply to a company's television, direct mail, and social media advertising. A company's deceitful speech, such as false advertising, deceptive releases, and misleading commercial speech, receives no First Amendment protection, thus can be restricted and controlled by the federal government. What does this mean at the end of the day? It means a customer can sue a company for false advertisement of a product and the company cannot claim that its speech is protected by the First Amendment to avoid being liable for damages of lying to the customer. There are other important limitations on free speech, such as defamation—which is a false statement that injures someone's reputation—and protections concerning intellectual property, meaning important items such as patents, trademarks, and copyright.

It is good to discuss these generalities of restrictions on free speech. As in later chapters, I will discuss business ethics, and we can play tennis on whether Walt and later the Disney company committed fraud and breached its ethical duty or whether all is fair in love and land purchases. But before we get to that, let us rejoin Walt and his experience being put on the spot. He has made his land purchases and set a date to make his big reveal, but unfortunately, Toto pulled back the green curtain and revealed the wizard too soon!

After years of planning and months of secrecy, the stage was set for Walt's grand entrance as the mystery buyer. All was set to be perfect, and a date was chosen to make his grand entrance. His plans were formulated, every i, j, and ü dotted. His formal release date for the information was to be the middle of November 1965 in a perfectly produced package developed by the cream of Disney's public relations team. But "the best laid schemes of mice and men" (quite literally in this sense).

News began to formally break in early October of that year, with an Orlando Sentinel journalist, Emily Bavar, finally piecing it all together and able to skirt any political suppression for its release. Once Bavar's article got into the hands of the newsies, the wheels sprang into action. Disney officials in Orlando saw the article in a hotel and called for Walt. The Florida governor receiving word that same day called for Walt as well. Journalists, angry at missing the scoop and wanting the next big word, called for Walt. All this attention may crush a normal person, but this was Walt's forte. The public was entering Walt's world, not the other way around. Walt never had an issue relating to the public, and the public was about to understand that.

The role of public relations itself is to paint a picture for the public, something Walt Disney was beyond a professional in doing, on and off the screen. T.D. Allman notes that every element of the Disney company played an integral role in projecting its image out to the public. "Disney's movies, cartoons and television shows, long before the term came into use, were informercials for his theme parks." Allman contends, "Each profit center [the various branches of the Disney company] helped produce a cybernetic impact greater than the sum of its parts, namely the belief that what was good for Disney, was good for America." However, what would be on display in Florida after the discovery of the secret was not the various profit centers of a company, but a man, one steeped in grandeur and learned in the art of show.

Walt and his associates needed to kick the tires and light the fires, but this was undoubtedly something Walt took pleasure in. One of my personal favorite Walt quotes was when a critic was noting to him that Disneyland in California was not finished at its grand opening, and Walt quickly retorted, "Disneyland will never be completed, as long as there is imagination left in the world." That is quite possibly one of the greatest public relations spins ever given. Instead of agreeing with the critic—noting they ran out time, more will come, or some other standard excuse—Walt created magic with his words. He took a negative, an unfinished park, and turned it into a positive. I cannot say for certain, but I believe that quote created an ethos in Walt and the Disney company. Walt's oft phrase "It will always be in a state of becoming" appears to have a relationship to Walt's statement all those years ago. As such, what was originally meant as cover for a theme park not being finished eventually turned it into an inspirational corporate motto. That is public relations magic.

Walt had to be careful with his big reveal, for commercial speech did not fully fall under the umbrella of the First Amendment until the mid-1970s. Commercial speech had been regulated to prevent harm to customers and fraud. Now, press releases in general are viewed in a more favorable light when it comes to lack of regulations than, say, a newspaper ad to customers, but still Walt had to be on point. He could not lie or misrepresent his goals, meaning there had to be an element of honest vagueness. But he also needed to be specific enough to appear genuine and generate excitement for his planned project. Without the protections of free speech and a year's worth of state-wide speculation as to the mystery land buyer boiling over, Walt's team needed to ensure they avoided any hiccups.

The first taste occurred at the end of October when Disney officials met with Governor Burns of Florida, who was fortuitously speaking at a trade conference in Miami. The Disney officials informed the governor that it was indeed Walt who was buying up the land for a massive new development. They even graciously, and intelligently, gave the honor of making the announcement to the governor himself. On October 25, 1965 the green curtain was officially pulled back. It would be a little over two weeks later when the wizard of Walt, himself, would finally take the stage in front of a jam-packed audience in Orlando.

As newspapers were proudly declaring "This is Disney's Land," Walt and his team were busy entertaining Florida political leaders in California with the undoubted aim to shore up governmental support for the endeavor, and perhaps lay the groundwork for the requests they would soon be making of Florida. The meat of the announcement would be coming via a press conference on the afternoon of November 15, 1965. There Walt would took to the stage to finally show the world what he had in store.

As to the press conference itself, a special thanks to Disney Historian Jim Korkis, who took the time to put together a transcription of that conference. Walt did not have a script entering into the press conference, which would most likely give any public relations agent fits. He spoke from the hip. At times, during the conference, Walt would not answer questions directly but continued his train of thought. He may or may not have been cognizant of the overwhelming desire from the community at large to simply know that he was building another theme park—the fabled Disneyland East, which is what many truly craved. What Walt did do was speak in vagaries with a dash of specifics and a sprinkle of that magical charm.

Walt's first inclination of his plans was he wanted to do "something" in Florida, more than an "entertainment enterprise." With the availability of land, he acknowledged that he wanted something "different and unique" from Disneyland in California (I can imagine eyebrows being raised in the crowd). To which Governor Burns, who was attendant as a sort of interviewer/moderator, responded with the question that was on everyone's mind: but "will it be another Disneyland…?" To which Walt basically responded no, dressing it up and noting there are certain things he refined through Disneyland and his work with the World's Fairs that he would like to bring over to Florida, but he likes to "create new things;" he wants a new concept. Governor Burns during the session chimed in with an acknowledgment that Disney attorneys would be working with the State of Florida to close some loopholes in order to move forward. Walt did not seem to respond to this and it appears it was simply a notation the governor wanted to get out. In this conference, we also have the mention of the name Disney World, but as with other items, Walt skirted the direct meaning of this. He contended that the name was meant to signify the project itself and everything going into it was essentially a Disney World, as opposed to a specific name for the new attractions.

The governor, for his part, did not let his constituents down as he continued to press Walt, in an endearing fashion, noting that while Walt said there would not be another Disneyland, there would be a family attraction at the core of all this, bigger and newer than Disneyland, "right?" Walt did seem to give in a little, but still maintained his vagaries. In fact, it was Governor Burns who ended it with a promise of grandeur, calling that day "The most important day in the progress and the future development of this state." It seems Governor Burns was doing his best Walt Disney impression for the crowd.

That covers the videos and transcripts I have been able to discover. There is additional commentary, however, that indicates more of the press conference took place and additional items were discussed. What continues below is what Walt Disney was quoted as saying; maybe you will have better luck than me at capturing the firsthand accounts of this, but as I relay here this information has been passed down through secondary sources. This is what Walt explained:

> I would like to be part of building a model community, a City of Tomorrow, you might say, because I don't believe in going out to this extreme blue-sky stuff that some architects do. I believe that people still want to live like human beings. There's a lot of things that could be done. I'm not against the automobile, but I just feel that the automobile has moved into communities too much. I feel that you can design so that the automobile is there, but still put people back as pedestrians again, you see. I'd love to work on a project like that ... Also, I mean, in the way of schools, facilities for the community, community entertainments and life. I'd love to be part of building up a

school of tomorrow … This might become a pilot operation for the teaching age—to go out across the country and across the world. The great problem today is the one of teaching.

Now, there is a great amount to unpack in these statements. We see Walt's desire to step into the realm of urban planning. He had the desire to build a model community that was focused on how people live. This press conference also revealed Walt's introduction of the City of Tomorrow theme to the general public. As such, we get the undertones of a futuristic theme to Walt's plans for the Florida property.

Walt also began his discussions about the desire for traffic control and the over reliance on automobiles. This is a sentiment that was shared by others who were developing visionary cities—remember Motopia from an early chapter. An interesting element is his choice of language, "pedestrians" as opposed to saying something like looking towards other modes of transportation. Theme parks are geared towards pedestrians; cities usually are not. While Walt was most likely speaking off the top of his head, it is an interesting word choice.

Another fascinating part is Walt's focus on education and the school of tomorrow. This makes sense, as Walt had experience and enjoyment in education via not only elements of Disneyland, but his animation and movie studios as well. Here I think two quick Disney education-based film examples are pertinent, one being probably the most well-known and the other being the most intriguing.

The most well-known one is *Donald in MathMagic Land* (1959). I remember seeing this film as a child and loving it. If you have an opportunity to watch it, I encourage you to do so, especially if you have young children. This Academy Award nominated animated short follows Donald Duck through a fantasy land of math. Donald learns the many uses of mathematics in art, architecture, nature, games, and sports. Poignantly, we learn in the film that mathematical thinking opens the doors to the future. The film ends with Galileo's quotation: "Mathematics is the alphabet in which God wrote the universe." Beautiful.

The second example is *Man in Space* (1955). *Man in Space* was more an episode of a Disney series than a stand-alone film. It follows the creation of the rocket ship, using live actors and scientists intermixed with Disney animation. The film then moves from the creation of the rocket ship to exploring what man's first trip to space would be like (keep in mind, mankind didn't set foot on the moon until 1969, over a decade later). Importantly, it covers such concerns as to the effects of space travel on a person both physically and mentally. It examines the effects of momentum, weightlessness, radiation, and even considers space sickness. What is truly fascinating is since the film was so engrossing and well thought out, both the U.S. and Soviet governments requested copies of the episode to show to their rocket scientists. As such, it is alleged that *Man in Space* helped pave the way to man's eventual first trip into outer space by both of these countries. Really remarkable, and it goes to show you why Walt was excited about the idea of a school of tomorrow. The reference to a "tomorrow" also reinforces my point about the City of Tomorrow, as we are starting to really get the theme being developed for the visionary community Walt was planning.

> **eXperimental Tip:** What can be visionary for some—can represent destruction for others. What happens if people are already living near the location of a proposed visionary city? This was one issue Walt would not need to deal with on a large scale, as he proceeded in a relatively unoccupied parcel of land. Professor of City Planning Vanessa Watson tackles the issue of those already living in the space of a planned visionary city in her work "African Urban Fantasies: Dreams or Nightmares?" Watson found towards the end of the first decade of the 2000s, there was a spark of private property developers looking to engage in urban renewals, urban extensions, and new satellite cities in Africa. Intriguingly, Watson found a movement for "future cities" (aka visionary cities) that included "an interesting mix of property developers, designers, engineering and infrastructure companies, finance and IT firms and those promoting urban sustainability." More importantly, Watson takes into consideration, "What the possible impact of these proposed urban interventions might be, both in terms of those currently living in these cities and those on surrounding land?" Watson had a dire warning, noting that while the architecture and confluence of new style cities may be intriguing for global market players, and thus middle to upper class citizens of the existing areas, she found "what seems most likely is that the majority of urban populations will find themselves further disadvantaged and marginalized." Is it possible to redesign an urban area and satisfy all interests,

taking into consideration those at the top of the financial class system and those at lower levels? Or will one level need to be spurned for the advance of other? It is a deep question, and definitely feel free to examine Watson's work on the topic for further considerations. An interesting wrinkle you can add to this is looking at Walt Disney World Resort's impact to the neighboring residents of Orlando. A useful book in this sense is Professor Richard Foglesong's *Married to the Mouse*. Additionally, you should take a look at music mogul Akon's plans to create a futuristic Pan-African smart city in Senegal (built in the spirit of Wakanda - the fictional, technologically advanced nation depicted in the Marvel cinematic universe). Akon City, as it has been referred, is purported to be backed by the Senegalese government and funded by unnamed private investors. Are we on the verge of an African EPCOT or Watson's fear? What assurances has Akon taken in concern to those on all levels of society?

As such, it appears that Walt gave them a taste of what was coming. A model community, a City of Tomorrow. The specifics he did not give, but he dangled out some really fascinating items to consider. Would it be a bigger and better Disneyland? What did he mean by a City of Tomorrow? What is blue-sky stuff and why is that bad? The crowd left that Orlando conference hall with more questions than answers, except one: Disney had arrived.

CHAPTER 6
The Business Plan of the Living Blueprint

Walt had garnered enough land and ingenuity to build a Kingdom of Tomorrow, as opposed to just a City of Tomorrow. However, one is dreaming the other is doing. Visionary cities are a difficult business to get into; for every Miami Springs that gets built there is a Motopia that never comes to fruition. Walt wanted to do so much, but all those swirling ideas needed to be collected and melded together. Vagaries would no longer do. Walt needed a plan for his new business operation, a business plan for the living and breathing blueprint of tomorrow.

Behind the scenes, work on Disney's Florida land had already begun. Construction companies were hired, engineers contracted, trees began to be cleared, and all this before the November press conference we just reviewed. Ideas were already beginning to cement as to the direction of the property. Some very important items still needed to be worked out with the State of Florida and the local governments in Orange and Osceola counties, but moves were already starting. To bring all of it together, Walt realized he needed to present his business plan not just to the public officials of Orlando and Florida, but to the world as a whole. As such, he began his last great production, the multimedia business plan presentation of the Experimental Prototype Community of Tomorrow.

Business plans, much like public relations, are not a chapter you will normally encounter in a business law textbook. But like public relations, it is something I believe you will find useful to discuss from a legal standpoint. Business plans represent a more practical element of where business and law meet. The importance is in the practicality, and it should not be overlooked. So let us discuss, shall we...

A business plan intersects with business law on several indirect and a few direct levels. As mentioned earlier, you could probably skim through a number of business law textbooks and not see a chapter on business plans. This is a shame, as it is such an important aspect in business.

Business plans often vary, but in a general sense they outline business goals and describe how those goals are going to be achieved. They are essentially an initial operational roadmap. They are used to not only gather the entrepreneur's thoughts, but also if investors or other early stakeholders need answers, the business plan should have them. The size and complexity of a business plan is controlled in part by the size and nature of predicated business.

Some basic elements included in a business plan are: (1) Executive Summary, the elevator pitch, if you will (listen, do you have a moment to talk about…); (2) General Business Description, a section such as this allows for an in-depth look at what the business is and will be doing, an elevator pitch on steroids; (3) Products and/or Services, what exactly is for sale? (4) Marketing, refers to how will a business get its ideas out there; (5) Operations, how will a business conduct its day-to-day operations; (6) Organization and Management, who will conduct those day-to-day operations; and (7) Financial Statements, Expenses, Capitalization, and Financial Plans, effectively $$$.

As far as the business plan's connection with law, a business plan needs to be cognizant of local laws in the areas it wants to operate. This includes, but by all means is not limited to, every single aspect of governmental regulation… unfortunate, but true. The specifics include acknowledgments of what licenses and permits will be needed for the particular business. Every business normally needs a tax permit or operational license from the local government where it operates, but some businesses need further licensure from the state—think, for example, of a bank or a nursing home. All licenses and permitting requirements should be outlined in a business plan. Additionally, the regulations or restrictions that may apply (zoning, for instance) should be detailed out. Then, of course, any employment issues that may arise, for example a barber shop needs licensed barbers. If a business plan runs afoul of the law, then the business it is planning has no chance of survival, well, except if you are Walt Disney. For if the laws got in the way for Walt, he simply needed to make sure they would change those laws (more on that later).

So that is what a business plan is. Let me tell you what it shouldn't solely be, and that is a market and/or feasibility study. In business development, there are two important early studies out there, market and feasibility. During the late 1950s and early '60s, Walt had numerous market and feasibility studies conducted by Economics Research Associates, a consulting firm, in search of the right land. The Disney company had agents conduct studies all over the East Coast, especially Florida, well before the eventual land purchases.

A market study looks at demand for a particular product or service and whether there will be sufficient interest from the community. A feasibility study then asks whether it is possible to make a financial and social profit in that particular market/location. These studies are preformed early in the process. While they can be referenced in a business plan, they are separate from the plan itself and often prepared by third parties. Think of them as source material that a business has created for itself. They are very important parts of business endeavors, especially large-scale ones in new markets.

> **eXperimental Tip:** The fabled bridge to nowhere. Market and feasibility studies help a business owner avoid building the bridge to nowhere. They actually play an interesting role in the U.S. immigration system. When a foreign business owner petitions to open up a new subsidiary office in the U.S., the U.S. government requests that business owner file along with their visa application a market and feasibility study. They do this one: to ensure that the planned business venture is actually real and the business owner is planning on opening a business in the U.S., and two: to determine whether that business will feasibly generate jobs, revenue, and taxable income in the U.S. The market study will show there is interest in, say, Brazilian-made soccer shoes in the Orlando community, and the feasibility study will show that a Brazilian soccer shoe store will not only make money by offering shoes at prices people will buy but also generate a social impact by hiring local employees and utilizing local vendors. This requirement is in addition to showing that the company will invest sufficient capital (money) and lease a sufficient space to operate. Do you think it is important for the U.S. government to require foreign companies to show they will be successful? Is it not simply enough to show that the company is leasing a space, investing capital in the U.S., and trying something new?

A market study is paramount for moving forward with design, investment seeking, and promotion. The market studies that Economic Research Associates conducted on behalf of Disney focused on the viability of various East Coast locations supporting a full scale recreational and potentially residential Disney operation. For example, the market studies showed that Florida's favorable year-round weather was more beneficial than, say, a New York site as far as capturing a larger percent of the tourist market on an annual basis, i.e. could make more money. In addition, the Economic

Research Associates' Florida feasibility studies focused on proximity to planned and existing highway systems, cost of land, topography (shape and substance of land), size of land available, and the number of people who owned the land. One study showed the location of two new highway systems could increase travel to what was at that time very cheap swampland. For Walt, this new merging highway system encouraged the Orlando site over other locations in Florida, such as Ocala or Palm Beach. Walt would share his market study with the architects, Disney engineers, and landscape architects who would eventually be charged with developing the property and reshaping the topography. Based on the designs, Walt and his brother Roy, the money man, would calculate construction and other project costs, as per the initial sources the Florida Project was looking to be well above the cost of Disneyland. The feasibility study would also test whether the expected revenues would generate enough to cover the expected costs and ensure profits.

For Walt, the market and feasibility studies had been completed, the news broken, and the press conference held. Additional feasibility studies would be conducted and shared even after the initial business plan was created for the benefit of community stakeholders to show the economic benefits of Disney's changing plans. At the time though, Walt felt comfortable enough with what he had to set further pieces into motion. Now was the time to move into the realm of the concrete. Revisiting sources, there appears to have always been this idea to build a City of Tomorrow, based upon Walt's interest in urban planning and his drive to create a brighter tomorrow. Evidence of this dates back to the late 1950s and the feasibility study drawn up for the potential Palm Beach, Florida location. But now was the time to take all those thoughts and lay them down in a succinct manner for public consumption. That task would fall on Walt's core team, but especially Marvin Davis and Marty Sklar.

Marvin Davis was charged with piecing all of Walt's ideas together in a cohesive form that could then be utilized by Disney's other team members, including Marty Sklar when writing the script for a visual portion of the business plan. Indeed, Walt was ahead of his time with his business plan, utilizing his movie studio production facilities to help anchor his public relations push. Walt knew he needed to include a visual element to his presentation. This was undoubtedly learned from his years of studio works and appearing in his own educational and art-based films. This was going to be another Disney Presents, but on a scale the world had not seen before. But first, he needed Davis to construct a business plan.

Davis had to reign in the dreams, designs, and specifications Walt had been collecting and espousing for years. Davis was charged with essentially being the dream catcher of the Experimental Prototype Community of Tomorrow. Walt envisioned a truly all-encompassing showcase for his Florida enterprise; Davis needed to outline and properly structure how a theme park like Disneyland, hotels, resorts, campgrounds, convention centers, the Experimental Prototype Community of Tomorrow, satellite communities, entrance areas, and even an airport, would interact with each other. This is in addition to the philosophical ideas that Walt wanted to include, items such as his reduction on the reliance of the automobile, the school of tomorrow, and figuring out what Walt meant with a general theme of "tomorrow."

Davis also needed to hone in on Walt's desire to integrate new systems. Walt was interested in showcasing the property through new transportation methods. Walt's concerns also focused on solving urban decay, meeting the needs of the public, providing happiness for the people who would be residents of the property and visitors to it, generating consumer desire, and as always open to being in a state of becoming. It was a formidable task to settle down all these swirling thoughts and ideas. Davis knew what Walt wanted, and he would try his best to focus it all.

Let's you and I take a trip into finding out what Walt Disney had planned for his Florida property. The abundance of land offered an abundance of options. After that we will look at how Marty Sklar would articulate those plans via a script for a visual film display of Walt's plan. To bring it all to a close, we will touch on a piece of the puzzle I have yet to mention.

What was Walt's business plan for all that land? Walt wanted to bring research and development to the proving grounds. Why wait years to see what was being developed by America's top companies? He wanted to invite companies and inventors to an area that would allow their products to be on display—to be seen, touched, and absorbed. The advantages would allow for a quicker dissemination to the world, a living, breathing tradeshow of American ingenuity of epic proportions. Walt wanted people to live in and visit the area. Managing this duality would be a challenge for Marvin Davis as well as for Marty Sklar in his visual aid portion. In written terms, I can best breakdown Walt's business plan for EPCOT with an acronym, ALTON (yes, I know, self-serving, but I am the author, after all). ALTON: *Attractions, Living, Transportation, Organization,* and *Nirvana.*

Let us start with the first A, *attractions*, shall we? At the end of the day, Walt's plans for his Florida land purchase was a commercial enterprise. The Disney company is not, and was never, a not-for-profit. It is a business entity that has bottom lines and visions of increased wealth. Any desire to remove that latent incentive from the idea of EPCOT is folly. As such, it should be embraced head on. This was another business venture designed to increase profit. It needed to attract visitors through attractions. One of the immediate attractions would of course be another theme park. The theme park was seen as a cash machine to allow Walt to exercise his other desires. From experience, Disney designers and engineers could build Disneyland East quickly. Furthermore, a Disneyland East could start generating money and jobs at a rapid pace. The theme park would most likely have a few surrounding hotels and resorts for guests to stay overnight, each of them themed and exciting in their own right. Even EPCOT would be a series of attractions. The concern of course was the viability of the enterprise and its execution.

Now on to L for *living*. Walt never was able to fully describe how EPCOT would function as a city with residences and residents, but at its most basic level it would be a living tradeshow of technology and promise. Walt envisioned an all-encompassing community with residents living, working, shopping, and engaging in a myriad of leisure activities all within the EPCOT zone. At the heart of EPCOT would be a single dense urban core with an innovative hallmark hotel, convention centers, internationally themed shopping districts, theaters, restaurants, nightlife, business centers, and residential aimed amenities. The internationally themed shopping districts and other leisure items would be fully enclosed, much like our mega-malls of today, but at a grand scale. The internationally themed shopping districts would branch out from the center hotel in a petal formation, each essentially a city block, and would include shows and live performers. A few of the articulated theme designs were countries such as China, Germany, the United Kingdom, and Switzerland.

On the roof above the shopping district would be an open-air leisure center, with water features, trees, and swimming facilities. Tying all of this central core together would be the Grand Emerald Disney Marquee Hotel & Resort (Walt did not name his central EPCOT hotel so I decided to, but sounds right, doesn't it?). It would be a hotel like no other, sitting in the center of Walt's Emerald City of Diz, open to residents, hotel guests, and visitors alike, featuring the top innovations in hospitality.

Beyond the hotel and internationally themed shopping district, the urban core would be finalized with a ring of apartments for residents and employees of EPCOT. Beyond that would be a radial Garden City with additional petals extending out for low-density, single-family homes and residential amenities. You can envision a bicycle wheel as well to grasp the concept, but a daisy also works. The Garden City concept was key, as each successive layer of the community would be immersed in greenways, or greenbelts, and parks and water features to break up the residential areas. The size and space in between the residential homes would increase as you drifted farther from the core. Interspersed in these residential areas would be community staples such as fire and police stations, hospitals, post offices, as well other preferred items including office buildings, theaters, a television studio, restaurants, and administration buildings. There was even envisioned separate satellite industrial and residential zones.

All of these apartments and residences would be outfitted with the latest advances in technology available to the public and, if Walt had his way, items the public had not seen yet. The residents of this living tradeshow would essentially be models, as tourists and visitors would be coming to see exactly how you use the washer of the future or what is Xofa (my own invented word, but sounds fun). The variety of housing from apartments to glacial estates would allow all sorts of technological developments to be at use. Variances of living would be on full display. The residents from early on were thought to not be permanent landowning residents, but temporary ones that would be changed out at intervals.[21] This would allow Disney an added level of control, for EPCOT would essentially serve American companies and innovators with advertising not only in the community itself, but also when the residents would leave the community. Allowing American companies to display, demonstrate, and have residents discuss their latest products and services while living there and again when they moved back to their real homes would be a big draw to gaining the sponsors Walt needed. For example, one can imagine walking down the Swiss block in the urban core and the EPCOT residents having lunch next to you are talking about how easy it is to move the Xofa from one room to the next. "What is a Xofa?" "Am I pronouncing it right?" "Is the x silent?" It is really quite ingenious.

> **eXperimental Tip:** Some Walt Disney purists may not be overjoyed at the use of the term "living tradeshow" to describe EPCOT, but I believe that may be from a lack of cohesion of thought. As I mentioned earlier, we cannot ignore the reality that Walt wanted to make money while simultaneously engaging in a pet passion. The Xofa conversation at the restaurant above is a perfect example of that idea. I would definitely believe the residents of EPCOT would be encouraged and would probably take joy in having discussions like this while mingling with Disney guests and visitors. If you have

---

21 There is some debate about this even within the Disney EPCOT team in the lead up to Marty Sklar's film. Even more confusing is some of the language used by Walt, and Roy in the years to come, alluded to permanent residents or was vague about their status (temporary vs. permanent). However, internal Disney reports show Walt was of the mind that they would be temporary.

the chance to meet enough Disney cast members, you will realize what I mean. There is a communal reverence and a base excitement to their work. This also gives us a chance to explore how a business might engage with its customers in unique ways. In 2010, on the weblog MetaFilter a user named blue_beetle observed that "If you're not paying for something, you're not the customer; you're the product being sold." This statement grew in traction as the wave of privacy and advertising issues soared from social media and smart phone/tablet gaming and app companies. I think it is a great exercise to unpack that statement and figure out what it means. This is always an interesting topic for me to cover— the realization that companies use our "likes," "thumbs up," and "hearts" as market research to find out what we like and then sell that research. Sometimes this can take up a much larger element like metadata being used on a grand scale, but microscale advertisers use your likes to then fashion advertisements they think you would like or target products towards your social media experiences. This can be as blatant as an ad on your timelines, or as subtle as luring you to like additional social media pages that have less apparent, but still present, sale functions. The idea being your likes and interests are being sold to businesses like a product so they can then market to you. At least that is how I discussed it in the early half of the 2010s. Has that meaning changed since 2010? What do you think? Ponder this and enjoy. I know I did.

Special note: I should note the global pandemic of 2020 had a drastic effect on Disney employees. A vast number of them terminated from employment that they cherished. This undoubtedly had a viable and somber effect on even those that remained. I sincerely hope this is effect is just a brief improvisation in the dance, and that one day my words will again be ring true of the majority of Disney employees.

Walt still wanted to go one step further with *living*, and that was the industrial park. He sought to build his own research and development park, developing not only Disney company products, but also encouraging other developers to join in. EPCOT residents would thus stretch beyond being made up of retail and service cast members, but would also include scientists, engineers, designers, and industrialists. This industry would be on display where visitors could come and tour the research park to see exactly how a Xofa is built and what makes it Xofa-tastic.

Living gives us a surprisingly good idea of what was contained in the radial structure of EPCOT, but how did people get around? EPCOT would allow Walt to include one of his real passions, the movement of people. Walt always had a fondness for model trains; he had one on his property in California that was big enough to fit single riders. He developed modes of movement such as the Monorail and PeopleMover for use in Disneyland. He was lauded for his park design and its constant means of guiding the movement of its visitors. This moving passion of his brings us now to our third letter of the acronym ALTON, T for *transportation*.

Like Jellicoe with his Motopia and other designers of visionary cities of the time, Walt wanted to remove dependence on the automobile that dominated the developing urban and suburban life. Walt felt the automobile had taken its toll on societal structures, and he sought to replace automobiles in EPCOT with automated mass transit systems. There were to be several levels of transportation in EPCOT. Walt did not want to remove the automobile entirely, merely reduce the reliance on it. Roads would be secondary, placed behind homes much like an alleyway, quickly joining a beltway that would then offer exit sites out of EPCOT.

There would be no direct above-ground car access to the urban core (unlike Motopia, which as we saw would present practical problems with its above-ground bridge model). So where would the car access be for the urban core? The answer is below EPCOT's residential areas, shopping district, and hotel center there would be two levels of underground tunnels; both tunnels would run the length of the entirety of EPCOT. Additionally, directly under the urban core, there would be warehousing for supplies and goods to be brought in and then funneled above by elevators. The tunnel level nearest to the surface would be for automobiles driving through EPCOT on their way to Disneyland East or for select parking below the Emerald Resort. The bottom level would be for trucks bringing products and storage for supplies to serve EPCOT. EPCOT would be devoid of any tractor trailers or service cars, as they would all be tucked graciously underneath.

The next prime element of EPCOT's transportation model would be the means of movement into and out of EPCOT proper through the use of a monorail. Visitors would arrive to the Disney property one of two ways: The first would be through Disney's very own Jetport to Tomorrow (my word, but again, fun), a fully owned and operated Disney airport for the property. Visitors could also arrive by driving and parking at the main Entrance Complex. After disembarking either at the Jetport to Tomorrow or the main Entrance Complex, visitors would then be able to access the foremost mode of transportation through the property, the monorail. The monorail would connect through the industrial park, EPCOT, and eventually Disneyland East and would stop at each location in centralized transportation hubs. The gem of the transportation hubs would be located right in the middle of the Grand Emerald Disney Marquee Hotel & Resort, where guests could disembark and check into the hotel or explore the internationally themed shopping districts before going on their way.

Some history on the monorail: It was first introduced to the Disney company by Alweg, a German train company. The monorail had been a feature of Disneyland in California for quite some time; millions upon millions of Disneyland guests had ridden on it at this point in our timeline. The monorail, with its use of single-track aqueduct overhead style line, was envisioned by Disney as a perfect tool to help reduce freeway traffic. The monorail could be built alongside existing highways without deep disturbance. It was a perfect transportation medium for EPCOT, as it was a product Disney wished for cities, urban designers, and local governments to purchase or license from Disney for use around the United States and hopefully the world.

Upon arrival to the Grand Emerald Transportation Station, a visitor would be introduced to the final main mode of transportation at EPCOT, the WEDway PeopleMover. It was a means of transportation that was specifically designed for EPCOT. Walt began formulating and processing the idea for the PeopleMover as early as 1964. It would appear first as a prototype in Disneyland in July 1967. The PeopleMover is a fully automated short-range transportation system. While the monorail would take visitors and residents from major hub to major hub, the PeopleMover was for short-distance usage.

The PeopleMovers in EPCOT would begin on a separate level in the Grand Emerald Transportation Station, and several would fan out like spokes in a wheel. They would ride overhead through the shopping districts, allowing visitors to get a nice tour from above the guests and residents shopping below. They would then "stop" at the office spaces, apartments, glide over the greenbelts, and then "stop" at various stations in the low-density residential areas, looping back around to perform the same trip in reverse. I use the word "stop" figuratively, as the PeopleMover was designed to be continuously running with a covered roof and doors that would open automatically. Visitors would embark and disembark onto slow moving walkways. It is really quite an impressive means of transportation. Walt even had a chance to visit a similar model that had made advances in accommodating the visually impaired. Everything would be thought of and would be in a constant flow. Visitors would mingle with residents on their way home or to work. Guests would be able to see all the new various housing in the residential districts from above.

Transportation was more a showcase than "living tradeshow." As much of the envisioned means and modes for movement within the Florida property and EPCOT were to be Disney-owned or created. While of course there would be Disney products, services, and ingenuity mixed in with the technology and industry in the "living," the point there was to also bring other American companies into the fold as well. Transportation, though, was one of Walt's passions, and one he would want visitors to absorb and encourage their local governments to invest in.

Speaking of local governments, that brings us to the fourth letter in our acronym, O for *organization*. Organization here refers to the Disney company's organizational structure as permitted by the State of Florida, and is above all else in the story of the Florida land purchase, the idea of EPCOT, and the eventual creation of the Walt Disney World Resort, the single most fascinating part. As such, organization will be handled in two later chapters,[22] but to give you a sample, please put on your thinking caps because I am going to discuss something special…district.

Disney World's special district status is what separated Walt's EPCOT dream, and the eventual Disney World Resort that took its place, from other such land developments, for example Curtiss's Opa-locka. Walt from early on knew rules would need to be bent to build not only a Disney theme park in Florida, but also EPCOT. That need to bend the rules is one of the reasons the Disney company courted Florida officials early in the process, flying them out to Disneyland to show what was needed. Specifically, Disney would require relaxed or modified building codes. If EPCOT was truly going to be in a state of becoming, more rules would need to be changed and adopted. This is especially so if Walt wanted to maintain the type of control a theme park allows him to have over a city full of residents.

Walt spared no time in getting his project moving; land use and development reports had been conducted. Disney's chief development officer on the ground General William "Joe" Potter, who had worked with Disney in the New York World's Fair and had experience in the Panama Canal Zone, knew that Walt would need increased control over drainage, land

---

22 Chapters 8 and 11

reclamation, and land use in order to avoid regulatory setbacks and logjams. Additionally, there were a host of other concerns: taxation, interference from Orange or Osceola counties, zoning, business licenses, and voting control once residents moved in, to name a few.

Ideas were floated to Walt by men such as Paul Helliwell and Ben Foster about the best way to structurally organize the Florida property. Paul Helliwell suggested setting up a new city on paper; it would give them advantageous control, but not to the full extent Walt truly wanted. Additionally, it did not preclude the Florida property from interference from the counties. It was Ben Foster and Tom DeWolf, an attorney from Helliwell's firm, that suggested a possible special district be set up.

Special districts are essentially independent, special-purpose quasi-governmental areas that exist separately from city or county governments and can have immense administrative and fiscal independent authority. Many special districts are unique and limited in purpose, for example swamp drainage. Special districts generate income in many ways, such as issuing debt, levying taxes, and imposing fees or charges for its services.

Walt, and eventually the Disney company, would test boundaries of what a special district was meant to be. Ben Foster eventually presented the idea to Walt of a special district and all the powers it could hold, but noted some powers it could not have, as those were reserved by municipalities. To which Walt effectively decried, "Why don't we just do both—a special district with a city inside!" The organization of the Florida property was born. We will revisit special districts in the chapters to come, and hopefully you are as excited to hear about it as I am to sit down and type it for you.

Last, but definitely not least, is our last letter, N for *Nirvana*. There was an ephemeral quality to Walt's plan for EPCOT. Nirvana, in its truest sense, is the absence of much and more, and while I am not a practicing Buddhist or a religious studies major, I did read *Siddhartha*, if that counts for something.[23] Nirvana, its deep meaning, or ability to embrace the lack thereof, is an important signifier in the Buddhist culture, an endgame goal. The term has been morphed by the outside world into a new definition, and when mentioned in common conversation can mean an ideal or idyllic place. It is the latter definition to which I am referring when I speak of EPCOT.

Why on earth go through the process of creating an Experimental Prototype Community of Tomorrow when it did not appear to be what people wanted? They wanted another Disneyland. Although Walt did not like squeals, he was in fact partaking in one, as Disneyland East was to be

---

23 In fact, Hermann Hesse is one of my favorite authors. I read his book *Demian* as a young teenager and it opened my eyes to what the literary world had to truly offer for those who are simply foolish enough to pick up any random book they see.

included in the program. More importantly, Disneyland East looked to be the first thing out the gate. There are tales of Walt's interest in city and urban design, his fascination and appreciation with the World's Fair, and his altogether favorite passion, trains and transportation. That all does seem to coalesce with creation and design of EPCOT. Walt was a businessman; he had diversified the Disney company from day one, starting with animation shorts, on to animated movies, and then into live action, all the while mixing and mingling with government and commercial educational programs, including Disney educational titles, eventually redesigning a film studio, designing a college campus, and then an entire theme park. All that does not even cover brand management through television programs and merchandising. Walt and the Disney company had almost done it all, and in fact the theme park had already allowed for Walt to explore his interests in transportation, as was shown with the advent of the monorail.

But, for Walt, it appears it was not what he had done but what he could do next. As I briefly mentioned in the retroventurism chapter, Walt built new ways and environments for people to have fun, to work, and to study. Walt now wanted to combine all those and show the world how they could live. Walt believed he could do it better and, even more so, turn a profit while doing it. Disneyland was built because Walt knew he could build a better theme park; he now wanted to build a better way to live. That takes guts and aspiration, something Walt was not lacking, but it also takes something more to bridge the gap, in that Walt believed he could make an enhanced community, just as he made a better theme park. There was an altruism in this, a legacy of hope. In fact, we can hear it in Walt's own voice when he declares as much in his last ever recorded film, "I don't believe there is a challenge anywhere in the world that's more important to people everywhere than finding solutions to the problems of our cities."

As to that last film, Marty Sklar wrote the script with the help of Walt to serve as a visual aid portion of his business plan. The film commonly referred to as the EPCOT Film was finished in the fall of 1966. It gives the best evidence as to Walt's proclaimed grand dream for the Florida property. It is coherent and offers more concrete motives than the accounts pulled from his first public relations foray in November of 1965. For example, it confirms the entirety of the area would be called Disney World and there would definitely be a full-functioning theme park. The theme park is mentioned early in the film, probably in recognition that it was what Floridians wanted to hear most. Walt also uses the caveat that EPCOT "will always be in a state of becoming." The video was to be played initially for Florida press and dignitaries and then would eventually be released for broader viewership. I will recount some special features of the EPCOT Film[24] and how they relate to Nirvana. With that said, let us hear from Walt himself utilizing the script Marty Sklar and he worked on.

The EPCOT Film features two main portions, one of Walt speaking himself about the project on either end of the video and a narrator giving additional details about EPCOT in between. Much of what Walt mentions is covered above in the business plan, but it is through his own voice that we really begin to sense what EPCOT was meant to mean, look like, and its role as Nirvana. Nothing can sum up the Nirvana like the nature of EPCOT better than when Walt says EPCOT will be a "living blueprint of the future where people live a life they can't find anywhere else in the world." Essentially, it would be the ideal community or idyllic place above anything else the world could offer at that time. That term "living blueprint" is no mere happenstance language. It is used again by the narrator as well, noting it will be the residents' responsibility to keep up this "living blueprint of the future."

As far as altruistic goals, Walt reinforces the concern to address the public need, advances in school education, and influencing generations to come. The residents, which Walt envisioned would number 20,000, would work in EPCOT, the Disney World theme park, and the industrial complex. The narrator notes how it will be a community with "employment for all." The film is careful to note that this "living blueprint" is not a standard community or city but is specifically a "planned environment." EPCOT is meant to demonstrate to the world what proper control of planning and design can do, essentially obtain Nirvana.

Eddie Sotto, an ex-Disney Imagineer, used some fascinating language to describe what it is to be a Disney company design team member. "It's a holistic approach to solving where big ideas lead to seamless experiences. Bigger breakthroughs that have human appeal. When people are happy they spend more." I personally find this to be one of the best explanations as to what Walt was trying to achieve with EPCOT. Walt was a businessman at the end of the day, but that did not take away from what he was trying to accomplish for the world. Walt was trying to break through our current idea of what a community could be, aiming for Nirvana.

> **eXperimental Tip:** "Words are, in my not-so-humble opinion, our most inexhaustible source of magic."
> Words from the great Albus Dumbledore (special

---

24 The video is currently available on YouTube. If the link goes bad, there are enough Disney fans out there that out versions should exist if you search for it. If internet no longer exists to be able to find another link, my presumption is you may have bigger questions being asked and hopefully answered than where the link to this film is located.

thanks of course to the person who wrote them, J.K. Rowling). The EPCOT film was a well-developed script written by Marty Sklar and approved by Walt. As such, these are important words that are contained therein. "Living blueprint" and "planned environment" are two great terms to unpack. "Living blueprint" is an interesting term. A *blueprint* is a guide for making something or a design to follow in order to make something. While *living* could connote that static guide will take on a life of its own with people moving about, or can it mean more than that? "Planned environment," while only mentioned once in the video, is an important one to me. I view the term in its totality. A garden is a planned environment. It is a human exercising control over nature. A theme park is a planned environment. Life and city living are not planned environments; they are forms of accepted chaos. The EPCOT Film's use of "planned environment" brings home what I believe EPCOT really was: destined to be a contrivance. I do not mean this in a negative light, but Walt wanted to build Nirvana, a picture-perfect world that would always be beyond the reach of every other living breathing community, an aspiration. He was putting on a show at such a grand scale that it would be hard to believe it as such. His Disney World is a stage and we were literally to be actors amongst it. It was meant to give people hope and make them yearn for more, so while it was a contrivance it was a beautiful one. I should note my idea is not a new one; according to author Steve Mannheim, community planner Ray Watson brought this issue up to Walt in 1966, questioning whether Walt was building "a natural community" or "an exhibit." Mannheim uses the word laboratory attraction when discussing this question. What do you think? Am I digging too deep...or not deep enough? Do you think Walt planned an actual real city, or maybe even a hybrid real city/contrivance, or a contrivance meant to appear to be a real city?

Walt also notes the importance of EPCOT and its adjoining industrial complex will be a platform for free enterprise, "a showcase of industry at work." Free enterprise was big on Walt's list, as was his belief in American capitalism. In fact, Disney was one of American capitalism's premier beneficiaries. But what he found to be the most compelling was the possibility of all businesses coming together to put on a show, and really demonstrate American exceptionalism to the world in this aspect. The entire EPCOT would be constructed in a way that would allow ease of change, as new products would replace older ones. This would reflect EPCOT's status of always becoming. Walt notes in the film that EPCOT was really the heart of everything Disney was doing. It would be interesting to imagine what it would look like.

Which brings me to that one item I have not mentioned yet, our third part of the business plan presentation: the physical. Walt Disney had always been a fan of models, and EPCOT could not exist without one. Walt charged Marvin Davis, with help from artwork by Herbert Ryman, to build a one-eighth model of EPCOT. The original model measured closed to 7,000 square feet. It featured approximately 4,500 buildings and 2,500 vehicles. It contained all the EPCOT elements, sport stadiums, jetport, underground passageways, and all the buildings mentioned in the business plan, including new ones such as a nuclear power plant. It was truly a massive undertaking, as the model itself was fully lit and automated with the PeopleMovers and monorail in motion, as well as buildings furnished and lit from the inside. The model premiered in Disneyland in California in July of 1967.

Walt would have been proud of the model no doubt. I say "would have" because Walt passed away in December 1966. He left a legacy as large as any person could leave behind. As Dr. Martin Luther King, Jr. rightly asserted, "So many of us in life start out building temples: temples of character, temples of justice, temples of peace. And so often we don't finish them." That would be the case with Walt and his temple of tomorrow. Walt would never see his EPCOT model finished nor the actual EPCOT either. The EPCOT Film in fact would premiere after his death as well. So many questions would arise after Walt's passing. Walt's brother Roy would pack up his own retirement plans and assume control of the Disney company, including Disney World. He would set that project on its new course and be in charge of some of the most intriguing aspects of the property that live on today. When one man sets down the torch, he does so with the hope that there is another who will pick it up. Roy picked up that torch, but in his own way.

As we learned earlier, Walt, with the help of others, prepared a multiphase business plan, using both visual and physical aids on top of a generally laid out business plan. It is really quite remarkable from a business proposal plan setting. As the Kauffman Foundation notes in their discussions on

GrowthVenture, "Over 80 percent of people learn best through visual stimulus." Thus, one can conclude that with excellent and varied visuals—the EPCOT Film and Progress City model, for example—one will improve the audience's level of understanding of a business plan. Walt was a master of the visual arts; this was his forte, and his mastery was made greater by bringing in some of the best and brightest visual artists, which can be reflected in the artwork and models created for EPCOT. This three-pronged approach, used on both the state and local government officials in Florida and the United States public at large, was a master stroke for shoring up what the Disney company had to do next.

eXperimental Tip: This is it! You made it! Congratulations. No, not the end of the book, we have so much more. Trust me, I'll have loads of fun in these next chapters and you will too, I have no doubt. This is it! means this chapter and the ideas presented in it is what lead me to using EPCOT as a teaching tool in my own college level classes. However, this chapter goes beyond what I was able to achieve. The project I always envisioned my students doing was a three-pronged business plan for a unique special district of their choosing. I only got so far as the first two, a business plan and visual aid, but I would have loved to have my students build a model as well. I believe all three really bring the idea to life, adding almost a science and design competition flair to the whole exercise. Hopefully, by the time you read this book, I am already doing that with students, but if not, I need you to take up the mantle. Heck, you can even do it at home with your friends, family, or pet parrot. This chapter is the backbone of what I envisioned, an all-encompassing final project of which I would sit in judgment of and admire the work completed by students. I will devote the epilogue of this book to this assignment and how I worked it out, but I wanted to let you know. This is it!! Great, let us continue.

CHAPTER 7
Regulations for You and Me

The void. You can stare at it. The question is whether it will stare back at you. Walt Disney died in December 1966. He left behind a thriving theme park in California, a healthy movie studio, and a plot of land the size of a small kingdom in the middle of Florida, while the Disney company's resources remained to finish the Florida project. Questions fermented, though, as to whether the will to complete it did. There is some speculation based upon retrospective quotes that after Walt died the idea of EPCOT was abandoned. Whether that is true or not, there was a moment when something was decided; was the move forward the theme park and resorts, or building the Community of Tomorrow?

As far as Walt's brother Roy was concerned, regardless of whatever plans sat in the future, the show must go on. As such, the EPCOT Film, as prepared, would be shown to Florida dignitaries and eventually to a broader audience. The desires of the Disney company moving forward would be projected under the visage of Walt himself. Which is understandable, as the man stood so tall and large, and Walt dreamt as big as dreams apply. As we proceed through this chapter, I wish to note that I have not been able to ascertain a definitive source on Roy's mindset in those early years after Walt's death, but his actions may actually be a more telling barometer than any biography on his life.

Roy kept with Walt's plan in the beginning. The first step was the presentation of the EPCOT Film. The benefit of the EPCOT Film is that it coordinated with Roy's initial vision, that a Disneyland East must be built, and built first. As mentioned, the EPCOT Film places an early emphasis on this; as such, being that Roy was a proponent of Disneyland East, this all meshed together nicely. The big question mark was EPCOT itself. From Roy's actions, as will be explored in this chapter, he wanted the State of Florida to concede all the powers it could to make EPCOT a possibility. Thus we enter the government regulations chapter.

So first, let us discuss a bit about how governments regulate business. Government interjecting itself into the means and operations of businesses is nothing new. As we saw from early chapters, governments are the ones that sanction and construct the framework of business enterprises. So how else, in the modern spectrum, does business and government regulations interact?

I can make a short list; there are more nuanced items, but this general list provides us with the tools to proceed. The six prominent items consist of (1) *Labor*; (2) *Commerce*; (3) *Taxes*; (4) *Environment*; (5) *Licenses and Permitting*; and (6) *Zoning*.

Out of that list I will punt one for later chapters.[25] Labor, covers the people living and working in EPCOT. The chapters that cover labor will include not only the nature of labor law, employment, agency, but immigration as well. So be patient, everything in its season.

Commerce, is of a different type than the others on the list. While it is important, it also catches all the items we have previously discussed, which are business formation, advertising, contracts, and consumer relations. Regulations and laws, such as false advertising, the Civil Rights Act, and the eventual American Disabilities Act fall under commerce. This branch of law generally reflects the exercising of the federal government's power through the Commerce Clause.[26] States can impact commerce as well through contract and general business regulation. A recent example of this is the business shutdown orders during the COVID-19 pandemic. Orders coming from the governor's office (Executive Orders) or those issued through the administrative agencies such as the Division of Business and Professional Regulation in Florida (granted authority through the governor) are examples of this. These are things the Disney company most likely could not avoid regardless of their setup. As Roy learned, while certain laws in the State of Florida could not be impinged upon in certain areas, they could be more easily changed in others.

Another topic that is tackled with ease is taxes. The piper gets his due one way or another. Taxes are a broad topic because it is the bread and butter of why governments interfere with business; they use the taxes collected to help support the governmental establishments. Taxes such as income tax, excise tax, employment tax, and sales tax are all collected by federal, state, county, and municipal governments. While Disney could not avoid most of these taxes, they could be manipulated, and one special early tax was extremely important.

Florida land is taxed at various rates depending on its usage. One of the most beneficial rates is agriculture. That is why you may see an occasional grouping of cows right smack in the middle of a city in South Florida. The landowner is taking advantage of a tax loophole. Instead of leaving

---

25 Chapters 9 & 10

26 The Commerce Clause is based upon Article 1, Section 8, Clause 3 in the U.S. Constitution. This clause gives Federal government the power "to regulate commerce with foreign nations, and among the several states, and with the Indian." The Federal government uses the Commerce Clause to pass laws over the activities of states and their citizens as those activities relate to inter-state commerce.

the ground empty, and thus fall into a different tax bracket based on eventual usage, the cows allow it to be considered agricultural land. Thus, lower taxes. Which, granted, is probably the best job a cow could have in the United States, so no complaints here. Once construction begins on a parcel of land that was agriculture, that land is taxed at the rate of what the ultimate development will become. This causes a headache for any long-term, multifaceted, grand-scale, multiple-year construction programs such as Disney World. So Roy sent in some of Walt's best men, including Paul Helliwell, to speak with the county tax assessors from Osceola and Orange counties. They were able to reach a deal to postpone much of the tax impact until Disney World was formally opened. This was the first sign that local and state government officials were willing to bend the rules, or even create new ones, to keep Disney World on track.

So that leaves us with environment, licenses and permitting, and zoning. These items were going to require grand thinking, but the end result would give Disney more than they could ever have dreamed of. Enough powers and rights to essentially craft whatever their hearts desired. The first stage would be dealing with environmental control and the establishment of their first special district. The Reedy Creek Drainage District was created by Disney through the use of the Florida court system in May of 1966. The Drainage District, which was a special district, would allow General Joe Potter the ability to continue his work moving massive amounts of land and water without much oversight. Disney would now be able to level the land upon which their grand experiment would be built.

But let us again revisit what a special district is. Actually, this time, let me let the Florida Department of Economic Opportunity tell you: "[s]imply put, special districts are units of local special-purpose government. Special districts are very similar to municipalities and counties (local general-purpose government). In fact, all three are more alike than they are different." Special districts are meant to be created for limited purposes, such as drainage in the Reedy Creek Drainage District.

Historically speaking, it is alleged that the great American renaissance man himself, Benjamin Franklin, created the very first special district in December 1736 (at about the age of 30). Franklin created the Union Fire Company of Philadelphia, which was a volunteer fire department. It functioned by having residents in a certain area paying a fee to receive services from the Union Fire Company. Many others in the city followed in Franklin's footsteps, establishing volunteer fire departments, leading Franklin one day to boast that Philadelphia had the best fire protection in the world. All brought upon by the ideals of free enterprise, as opposed to governmental oversight and control. I mention this because at the time that oversight would have been crown authority; as such it was a breakaway from this authority, maybe even the first step towards American independence.

The roots of special districts in Florida trace their origins to the early 1800s and have a connection with the establishment of Tallahassee as the State's first capital. North Florida had two main cities during this time, Pensacola and St. Augustine (each on opposite ends of the Florida panhandle). Whenever legislators wished to meet, they would have to go on a great sea venture to one city or the other by travelling around the peninsula. Key West during this time period was one of the largest and most active cities in Florida, and no doubt a stopping point for government officials on their voyages. However, this was travel cumbersome and perilous. In fact, one of the main money-making enterprises in Key West during this time was salvaging boat wrecks. The burdensome travelling led to the eventual decision to create a new city in between the existing North Florida settlements. Eventually, Florida's first capital, a log cabin simply large enough for all six of the legislators, was built in between Pensacola and St. Augustine, in what is today Tallahassee.

Along with the decision to build a capital, the legislators realized they would also be well served with the creation and maintenance of public roads to and from the cabin. The best method, they thought, to achieve this was allowing for the organization of citizens into a district with certain vested powers, including the right to build and maintain roads. Thereby the legislators authorized the creation of the first special districts in Florida by enacting the Road, Highway, and Ferry Act of 1822.

The next big step in special districts in Florida was in 1845 upon becoming a state. Several commissioners were afforded drainage rights, and to finance the project, special tax assessments were issued upon the landowners based upon acres owned and benefits the project would provide. The use of special districts continued through the end of the 1800s and into the twentieth century. With the Florida land boom in full swing in the early part of the twentieth century, remember our friend Curtiss, many special districts were created to finance large engineering projects. According to the Florida Department of Economic Opportunity, some of these special districts are still in existence today, including the South Florida Conservancy District and the Florida Inland Navigation District. We eventually see mosquito eradication districts, aviation authorities, hyacinth control, beach erosion, hospital, and fire control special districts grow into fashion. This is in addition to the continued creation and use of the traditional road, bridge, and drainage special districts.

Questions have always circled around special districts. To hand over power reserved for the state or local government to the hands of a private enterprise is an interesting transaction. Special districts have been surrounded in shadow and are sometimes criticized in this aspect. If you can recall Vanessa Watson's concerns about private enterprise activities with African visionary cities, that may be a good comparison. But, at the end of the day, their usefulness cannot be ignored when government is unable or incapable of acting. Furthermore, Walt realized the usefulness of this prior to his death, and Roy would explore all that Florida special districts had to offer.

There are conflicting views about how Disney wanted to proceed with Roy in charge after Walt's death. Internally, we know that the Disney team was focused on creating its dual system of control over the land via the creation of municipalities and overarching special district, as was presented to Walt from Ben Foster and Tom DeWolf. Furthermore, we know that, externally, Roy proceeded as if he was bent on fulfilling Walt's dream. The first big reveal remained the same, with the EPCOT Film premiering early in 1967.

Roy had to use all his expertise following the EPCOT Film, and have every available Disney player and partner on deck to push their plan over the line. What was the plan, though? Roy wanted to essentially convert the Reedy Creek Drainage District into a super special district. Roy would ask for the moon, and in turn would surprisingly be granted it. Roy had quite a few hiccups along the road to eventual success, this included a new governor being elected in the State of Florida and Osceola and Orange county officials needing extra assurances with each raising new issues along the way. But with each obstacle Roy was able to use Disney's sway and its cacophony of talent, including Paul Helliwell, Joe Potter, and a man by the name of Card Walker, who would eventually become CEO of the Disney Company.

For Roy, to get the powers he desired, he would not be able to stick with just the court approved drainage district. Roy would need to have legislation drafted to present to the Florida legislature itself in order to grant a law that specifically gave Disney what they wanted. Roy and the Disney team finagled, haggled, and negotiated their draft legislation. Disney proceeded to have the Reedy Creek Drainage District created under Walt by the Florida court system converted into the Reedy Creek Improvement District via an act by the State legislature of Florida. Essentially, Disney needed a new special law created for them that would remove restrictions of operations covering licensing, permitting, and zoning, amongst many other things. Additionally, this would coincide with the creation of two cities on the Disney property. All this was done with the idea of allowing the Disney company to build, unhindered by bureaucracy. Before I get to what powers Disney was given in Florida, a quick note on why they needed them.

A big need was of course building codes. We can take the point of view of a homeowner. Usually for a homeowner to put a new roof on her house she would need to contract a roofer. The roofer must obtain a building permit from city or county prior to operation. This takes time and is an extra step in the process, let alone an extra cost. Taking this back to Disney, any time Disney wanted to make a change in a ride for example, they would need to get a permit from the appropriate authority. If midway through the process Disney wanted to make a small change to the original plans, they may have been required to get another permit. That would have proven beyond burdensome, especially as we were not dealing with roofs but the possibility of highly complex attractions that, frankly, the local zoning code enforcement had little to no experience in dealing with. Think back on the eXperimental tip concerning Lex Mercatoria. Who is better suited for this job? The Disney company, who has experience in these particular attributes' safety? Or the generalized code enforcement team of the local government? Disney needed to cut out the middleman. Building and code inspections were a tedious element not required as far as Disney was concerned. Disney knew if someone got hurt on a ride, they would face litigation, so they knew they would need to be careful. They would also be establishing numerous different business entities to control all the different portions of the property, and the operational licensing and permitting and other bureaucratic requirements were thought to be unnecessary. And these are just basic items; Disney would need more rights to build a city with complex requirements. This is just a small example of why they needed a special legislation to create the Improvement District; what they were given is amazing to behold.

> eXperimental Tip: "I am never going to financially recover from this" – Tiger King. Government regulations coupled with liability. These are usually the two checks on a business. Government regulations provide standards to ensure that products are safe to use by the public and that services are described in an understandable way. However, the other side of the coin is lawsuits from the public against businesses. Lawsuits can even arise against businesses that comply with government regulations. For example, say government investigations of a new smart phone did not find out if it is placed within five inches of an open flame the phone can

explode. So, while government regulations said the phone was good to go into commerce, lawsuits later pop up against the phone company for the exploding phones. Is that fair? Will lawsuits that do not mesh with regulations result in unpredictability and confusion? This is a good question to flesh out, as it weighs the importance of both presumably predictable government regulation and the potential unpredictable litigation against each other. At the end of the day, the consumer receives two levels of protection from regulation and litigation, but this may also have a negative impact on businesses' desire to take risks, some of which may have been beneficial to the community at large.

The legislation that established the Reedy Creek Improvement District also affords us a chance to look at why Florida was so willing to give up control over numerous elements of governance over so much land. So let us look at the statute that created the Reedy Creek Improvement District, Disney's crown jewel of governmental experimentation.

The statute begins with several acknowledgements as to why it is important to make this law. This includes the affirmations that the "economic progress and the well-being of the people of Florida depend in large measure upon the many visitors and new residents who come to Florida," and this law is being passed "in order to assure the future welfare and continued prosperity of Florida." Thus the state legislatures had tied Disney's requests with the economic viability of the State. This was all done with the goal to keep Florida as a prime tourist and new resident destination.

What did Florida give Disney control over through the Reedy Creek Improvement District? It is a long and exhaustive list. However, to examine the scope and breadth of it, I feel we need to see all the elements. For this list of rights given to Disney, I use the title of the grant made by the legislator, as many of them are self-explanatory, but I supply more details where need be. So here we go, the long list of rights: (1) Legal Proceedings—this is a reference to its standing as an entity, similar to the business entities we discussed in the prior chapters; (2) Corporate Seal; (3) Ownership and Disposition of Property—this refers to their ability to acquire more land and also mortgage, control, convey, sell, and lease the land under their possession with or without consideration. I highlight consideration here because, as you will remember, for a contract to be valid it must contain consideration, as such the State of Florida is excusing Disney from this contractual element with regard to land transfers. Land transfers become important later in Disney property life with the Town of Celebration and the creation of Golden Oak. These are land areas that were returned to the county; (4) Lease Facilities—this section is mildly complex, but refers to the ability of Disney to lease or be the lessee of any of the facilities in which the Act grants to it. There are some restrictions, such as telephone and utility services; (5) Eminent Domain—eminent domain refers to the right of a government to take private property for fair and just compensation; this right was given to Disney[27] (6) Reclamation, Drainage, Irrigation—Disney was going to need to move land and water throughout its existence, and as such it needed to maintain this right that it had acquired when the Drainage District was set up; (7) Water and Flood Control, Erosion Control, Eligibility for State Assistance—this continues along with the ability to manipulate water ways and does not preclude the Improvement District from receiving State funds; (8) Water and Sewage Systems—this afforded Disney the ability to be a closed-circuit water supply and treatment system if it so desired. Being a closed-circuit would stop outside pollutants from entering or causing a shutdown of operations; (9) Waste Collection and Disposal—interestingly, Disney waste disposal systems in Walt Disney World are a technical marvel, with the use of underground utilidors that serve as corridors for Disney employees to move unseen and also house the Automated Vacuum Waste Collection system that uses pressurized tubes to funnel trash into repositories for later disposal; (10) Mosquito and Pest Control, Eligibility for State Assistance—may not seem like this would be needed, but do you know you need a special type of registered and licensed honey bee removal expert to remove or eradicate honey bees? (11) Airport Facilities; (12) Recreational Facilities—includes almost any type of recreational facility, some of the bigger ones are stadiums and museums. An interesting insertion but one that makes sense is also the facilities required to run television and radio broadcasting and ancillary items; (13) Parking Facilities; (14) Fire Protection;[28] (15) Advertising; (16) Transportation—this is a good one, as it mentions standard forms of transportation and the means to utilize them, as well as airplanes, helicopters, and monorails. The big one though is "other transportation facilities, whether now or hereafter invented or developed including without limitation novel and experimental facilities such as moving platforms and sidewalks." Additionally, Disney was given the authority to extend those modes of transportation beyond the Improvement District; (17) Public Utilities—another big one, as this is the nuclear power plant provision,

27 Recall back to Chapter 1, the right to eminent domain was one of rights given to early businesses by the North Carolinian government after the United States won independence.
28 A nice little throwback to the very first Benjamin Franklin special district.

78

Disney was given authority to build various types of energy producing plants and ancillary items. In addition, there is leeway for the "hereafter invented" as well; (18) Conservation Areas and Sanctuaries—they also had the power to stock areas with wildlife and promulgate rules and regulations for those areas; (19) Issuance of Bonds—Disney could now issue their own bonds. Bonds are essentially loans made by investors to Disney, which Disney promises to repay at a certain date with some additional payments during the course of the bond period; (20) Other Powers; Research and Development—a sort of catch-all provision to cover any ancillary items not specifically mentioned but would generally be believed to be required to complete any of the specific provisions. A long list, but it continues. In an additional section, Disney is exempted and excused from county, state, and other zoning laws. Disney is also given power over building and safety codes.

The law that created the Reedy Creek Improvement District is a ponderous tome in and of itself. The heart of it recognizes a desire by Florida to cement itself as a tourist state. With that in mind, Florida needed to take measures to promote conservation and the creation of vacation and recreational facilities. The Florida legislature outright acknowledged a need for EPCOT in affirming their desire for "residential communities of high quality and the utilization of the many technological advances achieved by American industry in developing new concepts in community living and recreation." This is a direct nod to the visionary cities movement that was occurring around the world at this time. The Disney company had struck when the iron was hot as far as this aspect was concerned. The Florida legislature was fully willing to grant Disney "powers and authority…to promote the development and utilization of new concepts, designs and ideas in the fields of recreation and community living." Disney was granted the ability "to undertake, sponsor, finance and maintain such research activities, experimentation and development as [they] may from time to time determine." That is a broad brush, but wait, there is more.

Disney also sought legislation creating two cities, Bay Lake and Reedy Creek. Reedy Creek's name would eventually change to become Lake Buena Vista. These cities were also afforded their own sets of powers and exceptions. A note about the list of rights granted for the two cities by the Florida legislature: unlike grants for the Improvement District legislation, each grant for these cities did not have a specific title attached to it. So when I list them below, I try and generalize them from their original text. There will be some crossover between what was granted to the Improvement District and to the cities themselves, though that was of no concern to Disney.

Let's get started. The list below includes rights given for the cities of Bay

Lake and Reedy Creek: (1) to acquire property and lease and mortgage the same; they could also dedicate streets; (2) to enter into third party contracts to effectuate their powers; (3) eminent domain; (4) to assess and collect ad valorem taxes;[29] (5) to invest in the city; (6) to borrow money for the city; (7) to issue business and occupational licenses and conduct professional registrations for businesses and occupations, in addition to collecting fees on the same; (8) to build and operate water and sewer systems, treatment facilities, and other ancillary items; (9) to build and operate waste facilities; (10) pest control; (11) to build and create airport facilities; (12) to build and own cultural, recreational and educational buildings, facilities, and projects of all kinds and description; (13) to build and construct parking facilities; (14) to build and own hospitals and research facilities focused on the treatment of disease; (15) provide police, fire, and sanitation services; (16) municipal employment; (17) advertising; (18) regulate and restrict use of lakes and waterways; (19) to build power plants, including nuclear fission and other new and experimental sources of power and energy; (20) build and own communication infrastructure; (21) to designate and maintain conversation areas; (22) to build roads, bridges, tunnels, etc.; (23) drainage and flood control; (24) to license and regulate the sale of alcohol; (25) to own and maintain cemeteries; (26) to build fire control infrastructure, as well as police infrastructure and designate police officers, vested with rights afforded to the police, such as to make arrests; (27) to develop and enforce rules on public safety, morals, peace, and welfare; (28) the right to adopt rules and regulations for road ways and air traffic; (29) build and own various forms of transportation and their associated stations, such as the monorail and experimental facilities such as moving platforms and sidewalks;[30] (30) pass ordinances to maintain the land owned by it outside its city limits; (31) to define and prevent nuisances; (32) the catch-all provision to include any other such rights for the health and welfare of the city or its inhabitants, but also the right to research, experiment and develop new technologies, and also mentioned here is the use of atomic energy for electricity; and (33) the right to issue bonds.

Now that was a list and a half, and this does not include their ability to define building codes and the requirement of all the administrative positions, mayor, city manager, and the like, which Disney was also granted. The Florida legislature also allowed for the creation of a municipal court and judge, who would have jurisdiction over anyone who violated an ordinance

---

29 An ad valorem tax is a tax on the value of piece of real estate or personal property at the time of the transaction.
30 Interesting that the moving platforms and sidewalks sound more like Motopia than Walt's EPCOT.

of the city, including criminal violations. The judge would be vested with powers to declare sentences and also issue warrants. Trials in this court would be without a jury, and appeals would then be sent to the State of Florida Circuit Court.[31]

Left off the table were schools. Disney did not gain the power to create formal schools, either through the Improvement District or the twin municipalities of Bay Lake and Reedy Creek. This is important, as the School of Tomorrow was one of the earliest elements that we can trace back to Walt himself in the November 1965 press conference. Even though this was a piece that Walt articulated, and one he undoubtedly was a major proponent of, the School of Tomorrow was not to be. Yet even without the School of Tomorrow, the municipal grant of power was really an extensive amount of rights, privileges, and ultimately responsibilities.

The cities would exist under the umbrella of the Improvement District. Roy had been able to secure for the benefit of Disney an immense amount of power. Their power befitted the amount of land they now controlled. Roy and the Disney team succeeded, at least in part, in keeping Walt's dream alive. Disney secured all the rights they would need to build not only a Disney World theme park, but EPCOT, the airport, the industrial center, and the transportations system discussed in the EPCOT Film.

Even more importantly, the rights were in perpetuity; forever. Florida wanted Disney badly, and most likely were afraid to do anything to scare them off. As such, there was no language written for oversight over all these powers (as with most special districts), or management if Disney got too big for its britches and negatively impacted the surrounding area. Florida saw the economic boom potential and did not want it to go to another state.

The laws had been set. The elected officials of Florida came to an agreement to grant an unprecedented amount of rights to the Disney company. Formal laws were set down in the annals of Florida in recordation of the agreement. It was truly a momentous occasion. To this date, the establishment of the Reedy Creek Improvement District represents the highwater mark of Florida special district status. Never since have so many powers been afforded to a private entity inside Florida.

> eXperimental Tip: All that control in the hands of so few. Walt's EPCOT, and even poignantly Disney's Improvement District and its twin cities, have some severe questions about its governance plans. As Richard Foglesong affirms, EPCOT represented,

---

31 One item I do not intensely cover is the U.S. Court system. I do urge a brief review of that to understand this aspect.

"Not democracy, but freedom from democracy." T.D. Allman notes, "Disney's legal experts next did away with representative government all together..." Alan Bowers notes, "EPCOT might have very well existed as a quasi-fascist city-state but I believe the temporary living arrangements would have diminished its effects." Walt wanted control over EPCOT, there is no doubt. As Steve Mannheim aptly leaves open, what that meant was never fully fleshed out by Walt himself, who was a staunch supporter of the American free market, democracy, and its way of life. It is an interesting dichotomy, between the man and the vision, that is worth examining independently. Outside of fascism concerns, though, the Disney company itself is often seen as the harbinger of a hyper-capitalist reality, with its cradle to grave approach to American consumerism. That determination may not be incorrect, but it is also worth examining on your own.

Everything was secured for Roy and the Disney company to move forward. Their first goal, as it had already been determined, was the development of the Disney World theme park. There would be some legal challenges to work out. For example, Disney, in its role as landowner, played an active role in one lawsuit against the Improvement District. This was done to find out if the Improvement District really was sound law. Essentially, suing itself to make sure it was okay against future attacks. Backwards, I know, but it worked. The Florida court system ruled in favor of the Improvement District, which further cemented its status. The challenge specifically focused on whether state-backed drainage bonds could be issued for non-drainage purposes by the Improvement District. As T.D. Allman notes, Disney's issuance of public funds for a private purpose was deemed permissible by the court. This was determined by the Court, even though the Improvement District was not directly related to drainage, because once Disney World was operational, the benefits of the District would inure to the numerous inhabitants there. Allman points out the problematic issue with all this, is that there would never be numerous inhabitants, a topic we get into further in our next chapter.

CHAPTER 8
Ethical Dilemma: "Walt's Gone"

E thics. As with many philosophical ideals, I can tell you what it isn't probably better than I can tell you what it is. Ethics are not laws, regulations, or ordinances, but laws, regulations, and ordinances can be based on ethical considerations. Ethics are not religion, but religions can contain moral ethics. To search for a definition, it is probably best I turn to an expert. The Australian philosopher C.A.J. Coady defines ethics as something that "should form a vital part of the body of knowledge we have and continue to seek about the most sensible and sustainable answers to the question 'How should we live?'" To take that into the business law umbrella, Coady may say ethics should answer the question "How should we conduct business?"

Business ethics are a mainstay in most business law textbooks. It is an important topic, as ethical considerations are both meaningful in business decisions, but also as a tool towards making business law entertaining. I believe that is a reason why it is usually found early in many business law textbooks; start with the fun stuff. Well, I for one believe we have been having fun this whole time, and this chapter will just keep that streak going.

Business ethics relate to relationships, and specifically the relationships a business maintains with its stakeholders.[32] How does a business treat those that have some level of interaction with it? If it cuts wages to its employees for higher dividend payments to its owners, is that unethical? If it pollutes a river in order to cut costs and pay its employees more as well as offering them health insurance, is that unethical?

> eXperimental Tip: If sewage is dumped and no one is around, does it still pollute? There is a term called Corporate Social Responsibility, which focuses on a business's contributions to sustainable development by taking active steps to deliver economic, social, and environmental benefits for all stakeholders. As we have seen previously, satisfying all stakeholders may be a nigh impossible task to request of a company. We also discussed in a previous eXperimental Tip what Machiavelli would think to do. But, one could argue, it is in fact much easier to mildly disappoint all stakeholders and actually achieve more long-

---

32 If you need a little refresher on that term, take a trip back to the public relations chapter.

term sustainable development. For example, if the business owners, customers, and environmentalists are all mildly upset with the activity of a business, but none of them are out right horrified, then that may be the best outcome for everyone. What do you think, better everyone is a little mad than one party furious and the rest happy? A quote by author and comedian Larry David to consider: "A good compromise is when both parties are dissatisfied."

To gain a clearer understanding of ethics not being the law, a good example is employee relations. If a business fires an employee for being late one time, most reasonable people would consider it unfair, maybe even unethical, but it is not illegal in a standard employee/employer relationship. Another example is employee uniforms. Some employers require their employees to purchase their uniforms or other items from the employer at a reasonable or even discounted rate. This is not illegal; it may be a little mean-spirited and money-hungry on the part of the employer to charge for this, but it may not rise to what most of us would call unethical. What if the employer over-charged for the uniform, above what it would reasonably cost? Now we start moving into the realm of unethical, even though it still would not be illegal.

eXperimental Tip: A provocative ethical dilemma is that of sweatshop labor. The term sweatshops is often used to refer to foreign factories that have poor working conditions, unfair wages, unreasonable hours, child labor, and a lack of benefits for workers. But to some economists the term has been unfairly applied in this era of globalization to any factory used by a corporate giant (think of your large tennis shoe, clothing, or electronics companies) not located in a post-industrial country. When one hears of a laborer in a factory owned or effectively controlled by a corporate giant in a pre-industrial or industrial country being paid $0.12 a day for working 10 hours a day six days a week, it sounds horrific, sounds unethical. What if you were to learn that the actual average salary in the country is $0.06 a day, and the average person works 12 hours a day for seven days a week? Does that change your mind on whether the corporate giant is acting ethically or not? If you find it entirely unethical, the corporate giant could refuse to engage in that country, but that means those double wage earners would lose their job. A long-term question of ethics would be whether the increased wages and reduced labor hours being offered are sufficient to encourage sustainable development for the employees and their families. If it is not, if the extra money is somewhat helpful but not enough to increase the employees' socio-economic conditions, the use of the sweatshop could then be still seen as unethical, even amongst globalists. These are good questions to delve into even in a personal understanding of how globalization works, or in a classroom setting of how to contextualize ethics.

Ethics become a little bit trickier with customers. For example, a business cannot engage in fraudulent advertising. For example, putting a newspaper ad that all TVs in an electronic store are 50 percent off, but when the customer arrives it turns out that they were only 25 percent off. That would most likely be considered both unethical and illegal. As such, ethics and illegality can overlap. How do businesses play with ethics in advertising? With statements such as "select TVs 50% off" and then the store makes one brand 50 percent off and the others all normal priced or even with higher mark-ups. When the customer arrives at the store, it turns out there was only a small number of sale TVs. This may be considered unethical, but the business did not do anything illegal, as it did say "select." This is, in fact, a common practice for most big box commercial retailers in the United States. It is also a great example of the difference between ethics and the law.

The law is usually seen as the lowest common denominator. A business cannot break the law, or, I should say, should not break the law. If it does there will be consequences. Ethics are a standard above the law, even though they may connect at times, such as fraudulent advertising. Ethics are how we would like a business to behave—honest, nice to the environment, cognizant of social issues. However, it may be irrational to expect a business do that in a capitalist society. If a company can earn more money by appearing to be socially responsible but actually not be, it would behoove it to do so for the sake of its owners and some of its employees. Or as Mark Dimmock and Andrew Fisher posited under one branch of business philosophy, "If, by lying, a business produces more happiness than by not lying, then it is morally acceptable for the business to lie." These are some of the ideas that we carry into our look at Walt and the Disney company's activities in the development of Walt Disney World, and examining those activities under the lens of ethics.

There are a few decisions made by Walt, Roy, and the Disney company in the earlier chapters that are worth exploring under an ethical lens. Those decisions are Disney's initial secret land purchase and, ultimately, the fact that EPCOT as dreamt by Walt and utilized by Roy was not built as detailed in the EPOCT Film and Progress City models. There would be an eventual EPCOT Center, now renamed Epcot, built in the Walt Disney World Resort. A prototype of the City of Tomorrow it is not.[33]

One of the very first ethical dilemmas Walt faced was how the Disney company learned about the land south of Orlando in the first place. As we may recall, a young Disney associate named Bill Lund first learned about the south Orlando tracts of land from a real estate broker David Nusbickel, of Florida Ranch Lands real estate company. Lund never informed anyone at Florida Ranch Lands he was with Disney. Nusbickel gave Lund materials on the Demtree Tract. Additionally, Nusbickel told Lund about the Bay Lake Tract and the Hamrick Tract. Nusbickel tried and tried to follow up with Lund, hoping of course to score a big pay day with his 10 percent commission on the sale, but talk fizzled out.

Lund on the other hand returned to California and presented his findings to the Disney company. These documents pushed Central Florida further into focus for Walt. Disney still did some last-minute searching in other areas but did in fact settle on the land Nusbickel presented. The problem arises in that Disney did not go back to Nusbickel to finalize the deals. Disney went with Roy Hawkins, Disney's hired real estate guru. Hawkins did partially engage Florida Ranch Lands in some of the real estate deals eventually executed, but Florida Ranch Lands either only got half commissions on some lands or outright none since Hawkins was initiating the transactions (as opposed to Florida Ranch Lands directly).

The issue came around when Chuck Bosserman, a salesman at Florida Ranch Lands, was invited, along with 18 other local Orlando officials, to Disneyland in California after news broke of Disney being the secret land purchaser. Disney conducted this venture to show off Disneyland in hopes to secure favor with local officials. While on the plane to California, Bosserman saw some brochures that had the name William Lund on them. Bosserman had met Bill Lund two years ago when Lund first came in to meet Nusbickel and always wondered what happened to the young man. Bosserman would <u>soon learn that </u>William Lund was in fact the same secretive Bill Lund.

33 Do not feel too down about this; in fact, many of Walt's plans found their way into various elements built in Walt Disney World Resort, not just centered in Epcot alone. We will explore some of these as we go along in later chapters.

Once in California during one of the Disneyland presentations, Bosserman came face to face with Lund, and it all began to click. Bosserman eventually returned to Florida and filled in Florida Ranch Lands' higher ups that Disney had done an end and around using Hawkins instead of Nusbickel.

The Florida Ranch Lands' owners were mad. Disney cheated them, they felt. Disney had acted unethically! For Disney's part, this "end and around" activity was probably not done to save a dime. As professor and author Richard Foglesong contends, it may have just been a result of the overall secrecy involved in Disney's entire operation. It still left a rotten taste and big hole in Florida Ranch Lands' pocket. Florida Ranch Lands eventually filed suit against Disney, and the case was settled out of court. Discussing this lawsuit does bring up an additional ethical dilemma: that of all the shadow entities used to purchase the Disney land.

Now, there is nothing illegal in the way Disney purchased the land using various corporate entities. The sellers were most likely comforted with getting the price they wanted for the land and did not care about who may actually be on the backend of all of this. But the prospect of getting more money for land, and knowing it was Disney, probably aggravated the sellers later. Disney's activities make definite business sense for Disney. The price for the land would have skyrocketed if word had gotten out that it was Walt pulling the strings. This also means Disney was beginning their relationship with Florida by avoiding, as Richard Foglesong puts it, "public accountability." That is in addition to misdirecting, if not indirectly misleading, the sellers of the property.

> eXperimental Tip: Does a rose by any other name smell just as sweet? What do you think about the use of the shadow entities? Is it acceptable to shield one's identity from the public to save vast amounts of money? Should a seller know who a buyer truly is? What if, for example, a particular seller had a moral objection to selling to large companies, and now they found out that's exactly who they sold to. Effectively, the sellers in Disney were robbed of that chance to exercise a choice based upon a full set of facts. Was it unethical on the part of the Disney company? You be the judge.

The land purchase and commission issue were also just a precursor, a ripple in the stream if you will, as to what was coming next down the ethical pipeline. Throughout the late 1960s, Walt, and subsequently Roy, insisted to the public and local and state officials of Florida that the Community of Tomorrow was a central part of the plan for the Florida property. They did this even though the public was more interested in a Dinseyland East. In furtherance of the EPCOT plan after Walt's death, Roy had shown the EPCOT Film to the Florida legislature prior to the Reedy Creek Improvement District's law being enacted. The problem is, of course, no Community of Tomorrow, with its 20,000 residents, was ever built. The real question behind that is when was the plan abandoned? This is a gray area, and one, according to most sources, Disney never clarified as to why or when the plans were fully abandoned.

This becomes an ethical question based on the timeline. If the plans to stop EPCOT were before or right after Walt died, all that occurred, for example, requesting all the rights and powers to build EPCOT, was done ingenuously or as an outright unethical fraud. Some secondary sources, such as T.D. Allman and Foglesong, alluded to the idea that there never was going to be an EPCOT. As Allman proffers, the Disney company needed to portray the idea of building a city so that they could obtain all the special privileges from the State of Florida. Allman dates this back to Walt himself. This speculative position comes from an internal memo Walt marked up, showing he did not want permanent residents, just temporary or tourists.

According to other sources, after Walt's death, Marvin Davis, who assisted Walt in developing the EPCOT business plan, attended a meeting with other top team members. These other team members included Roy, Card Walker, and Disney transportation specialist Robert Gurr. The topic of the meeting was the next steps for the Florida project. This meeting most likely represents the true birthplace of the Walt Disney World Resort as we know it. It was Roy who would formally change the name of the Florida project from Disney World, to Walt Disney World, in honor of his brother.

In retroventurism terms, this is a *regrouping summit*, where team members devoid of their past central authority figure and/or structure must regroup and move forward. Depending on the strength of the group, the plans laid down by the past central authority figure, and any external outside factors, the regrouping summit can either carry on the wishes of the predecessor, create a new vision out of the old plans, or abandon the project all together. It appears that Disney's regrouping summit occurred shortly after Walt's death, which is important, for it stabilizes the momentum. A lull or a failure in having a regrouping summit will most likely cause a project to collapse.[34] It is during this time we begin to hear allegations of outright unethical behavior on the part of Disney. According to some secondary sources, as interpreted by

---

34 We saw this occur with Opa-locka and the death of Glen Curtiss.

statements from Davis and Gurr, it was at the regrouping summit where the plans for EPCOT died. In fact, author Sam Gennawey states "[t]hat was the end of Walt Disney's experimental prototype of tomorrow."

This opinion, and ones that follow Gennawey's, seem to stem from possibly two sources as far as I can determine. Davis, as it is told, specifically recalls, after giving an overview of where the EPCOT project stood to begin the regrouping summit, Roy turned to him and said, "Walt's gone." Additionally, in a 2015 *Esquire* article, it is noted, "Gurr recalls one particularly devastating headline published in the wake of Walt's death: 'Epcot Died Ten Minutes After Walt's Body Cooled.' Interestingly enough, that sentence in the *Esquire* article is then followed by the statement, "[w]hile not entirely accurate…" It is unclear if that "not entirely accurate" refers to EPCOT dying or that there was no such headline at the time. I have not been able to independently verify the existence of this headline. Furthermore, while Gennawey is undoubtedly quoting Davis correctly, it is unclear if Roy was actually sending EPCOT out to pasture.

I say this for several reasons; one is that as far as the outside world knew, EPCOT was still a go. In May of 1967, the Florida legislature passed the Improvement District law, along with creating the two cities of Reedy Creek and Bay Lake. Additionally, in July 1967, the Progress City model was completed and put on display. Disney was still arguing the Reedy Creek Improvement District case before the Florida Supreme Court, which was not resolved until November 27, 1968. In that decision the Florida Supreme Court made reference to Disney's properties eventual numerous inhabitants; undoubtedly this opinion originates by Disney's attorneys arguing that EPCOT was go.

Furthermore, Roy is quoted in a 1970 promotional booklet titled "Preview Edition – Walt Disney World." In it he states that the work they are doing to complete Phase 1 (referring to Magic Kingdom and its associated resorts and ancillary items) "will provide immense knowledge for our organization as it assumes the challenge of creating the Experimental Prototype Community of Tomorrow in future years." Additionally, Marty Sklar was charged with developing the internal language for EPCOT Building Code in 1970. The code language includes references to "encouraging American industry, through free enterprise, to introduce, test and demonstrate new ideas." This language mirrors the EPCOT Film language.

All this is followed up by statements made by Roy in 1971 to *Business Weekly*, in which he noted the development of residential lots on the property would eventually get them to "the whole EPCOT idea." Finally, the most telling of them all was when a member of the original regrouping summit, then-CEO Card Walker, called Marty Sklar and asked him, "What are we going to do about EPCOT?" The year of that call was 1974. Following that phone call, a series of conferences and meetings (the final regrouping summit of Walt's original EPCOT idea) were set up with original and new team members to figure out what to do with EPCOT.

Among those members in the 1974 final regrouping summit was Davis and Gurr. Gurr is reported saying, "so we literally started in where we all thought Walt left us with ideas." I bring this particular statement up because this statement seems antithetical to the first Gurr quote I mentioned earlier, where he recalls seeing the headline about EPCOT dying right after Walt's death. It appears core Disney members as late as 1974 were vested in EPCOT. However, it was in this final regrouping summit for the EPCOT planning groups that reality began to set in. As Davis would note, without Walt the plans would have only gone so far.

Author Steve Mannheim conducted an interview with John Hench, a premier Disney team member from the 1930s who also would go on to help craft EPCOT Center in Walt Disney World. Hench related to Mannheim some of the issues that he and Sklar faced during the final regrouping summit—things such as engineering issues, cost, voting rights, and even legal issues arising with prototype products that were supposed to be developed and/or used at EPCOT. From my sense, it was at the final regrouping summit where EPCOT, as envisioned by Walt, finally gave way to what would become EPCOT Center, and now Epcot.

The mention of voting rights is an interesting one because of a 1968 U.S. Supreme Court case *Avery v. Midland County*. This case raised potential issues about the effect of having residents in EPCOT, regardless of land ownership. Per *Avery*, Disney may have been forced to give residents (temporary or permanent) voting rights. As Chad Emerson notes, "In light of the *Avery* decision, if Disney chose to allow individuals to reside within the District or its municipalities, doing so could require that the company extend to them voting powers in order to comply with the Equal Protection Clause." This could potentially dilute Disney's full control over the Improvement District or its cities. This issue was in fact unsettled in *Avery* if this determination applied to special districts or Disney's unique Improvement District. Interestingly enough, it would eventually not apply to special districts years later, but it is unknown whether it could apply to Disney's Improvement District or the cities laying underneath.

So we have several dates to contend with about when Walt's EPCOT idea was left behind and a new plan cemented (I'll call it the Decision Date). The earliest Decision Date is most likely at the end of 1966, right after Walt's death, coinciding with the initial regrouping summit. If EPCOT was indeed abandoned then, Roy and the Disney company's actions following that Decision Date are at their most unethical and, in fact, could be determined as downright fraudulent, especially with Roy proceeding before the Florida legislature with the EPCOT Film. That is a heavy charge to lay on the hands of Disney, regardless how you feel about them as company. One item I use for clarification is that I cannot speak to the mindset of Roy at this time. Our best evidence is his actions. Per his actions, and his statements in publications and interviews, EPCOT was still a go, though it was mostly likely not a priority for him, as he wanted to get Magic Kingdom (Disneyland East) up and running as Phase 1 of the project to start bringing in revenue.

The next possible Decision Date is 1968, after the *Avery* U.S. Supreme Court decision. This date might make some of the actions by Roy and the Disney company unethical, but I would not call them outright fraudulent, for the laws creating the Improvement District and the cities of Bay Lake and Reedy Creek had already passed. While *Avery* was decided prior to Disney's own *Reedy Creek Improvement District v. State* case, it was unclear if *Avery* would truly prohibit Disney from having residents in EPCOT. At most it would deem it risky, or potentially unwise, but it was not a formal prohibition against having residents. If the Decision Date occurred right after *Avery*, Roy and the Disney company's statements after that, if made with the knowledge that EPCOT may not be going through, would be unethical. This is because of Disney continued to use language in the *Reedy Creek Improvement District v. State* case that supported the idea that residents would be there when they may have held contrary internal discussions. However, it appears they had not decided to abandon it just yet, as per Roy's decision to render land plots and statements made during this time about continuing with EPCOT after Phase 1 was complete.

The last Decision Date would be the 1974 final regrouping summit called by then-CEO Card Walker, and headed by Marty Sklar and John Hench, amongst others. It is here that we see the dream of Walt's EPCOT unravel. This Decision Date would place the least amount of unethicalness at Disney's doorstep. The Disney team were, unfortunately, too far removed from Walt's original plan, which was last laid out almost a decade before. There was not enough steam without their conductor Walt. Additionally, Roy by this time had passed away after the successful opening of his last gift to the Disney company, Walt Disney World's Magic Kingdom and its associated resorts.

eXperimental Tip: So were people going to actually live at Walt Disney World or what? Try and research this matter on your own. It is an interesting question, and depending on the sources you read and the information that is deemed important to you, you may come out with different levels of Walt and Disney's ethicalness. One item focuses around whether Walt insinuated that residents of EPCOT would be full-time residents or part-time. According to some, Walt's discussions with the press and the EPCOT Film seem to say full-time residents; I do not get that impression directly. I think it is clear what Walt was in fact selling, but maybe I am speaking with hindsight. What do you think?

For what it is worth, I am of the 1974 Decision Date camp. I personally believe Roy was just not as interested in EPCOT as Walt was. And though Walt said he was not aiming for the blue-sky stuff, he truly was, and he most likely did not impinge that upon Roy. Roy postponed retirement to ensure Walt's Florida project could survive and thrive, and the way to do that was to focus on building what the people wanted, another Magic Kingdom. I believe Roy respected his brother and his brother's gravitas not only with the public but within the Disney company as well. Enough so not to outright quell EPCOT, but to postpone it until Roy got done what he needed to get done. In fact, it appears Roy summoned all his life force to make it so.

We will never know if Roy would have been the one to make that call to Marty Sklar after the completion of Magic Kingdom because Roy passed away shortly after its completion. Walt Disney World opened on October 1, 1971 and Roy passed away that December. Roy took Walt's plans and materialized them in part and set the property on the path to prosperity. If Roy had lived, it would give us an answer as to what his true thoughts were on EPCOT. Magic Kingdom needed to be built first, of that there was no question even for Walt. If Roy had lived and never made the call to build ECPOT, that would most likely mean the plans were abandoned either in 1966 or 1968. But now we are in the area of speculation, and regardless, Roy succeeded in his mission overall. Roy ensured his brother's dream would open and left it to others to continue the path.

CHAPTER 9
Employees of Tomorrow, Today: Part 1: Lexes

Employment law is a topic that pops up with some frequency in business law books. It is also a big part of many people's lives. It is so engrained in our society that I wanted to cover it here, as well. Employment law gives me a wonderful chance to explore what it means to work at Walt Disney World and what it would have meant to work in EPCOT if it had been constructed using Walt's vision. Employment law covers the relationship between a business and the people it hires to perform duties for that business. As such, employment law is much like public relations law, as it is where the contextual (the business) meets the tangible (the employee). I want to give you a good base structure on employment law prior to us taking a journey into the "what is" of Disney's employment structure and the "what ifs" of a retroventurism look at who would have actually lived and worked at Walt's EPCOT. Thus I have broken this chapter into two parts; first we learn the lexes (or terms), then we experience time travel.

Employment law is a very expansive topic and is a separate course in many business and law schools. It is often joined with agency law. Agency law covers the general relationship between a person (the agent) that acts on behalf of another person or entity (the principal). Employees fall under this. We are going to be taking a bit of an employment law train ride (or monorail ride, if you will) in this chapter. We will stop at the major stations as we move along on the route. As always, feel free to explore various items on your own with additional resources. This scenic tour will give you a foundational understanding. Mind the gap!

The relationship between a business and the people it hires is covered on two main governmental levels, federal and state. The federal government utilizes its right to regulate this relationship through powers afforded to it via the Commerce Clause. Using this power, the federal government regulates the treatment of those people who are hired to perform services for a business. Employment law is also a generally relatable form of the law, as we as people have usually been either an employee or hired someone to work for us. Let's you and I pull up to the first station, that is the "You're Hired" station.

An individual who performs services for a business is classified in generally one category or another, and those two categories afford the individual specific protections or obligations. The categories are "employee" versus "independent contractor." An employee is afforded multiple protections under federal law while an independent contractor is not.

Protections are a reference to rights that an employee gains by virtue of the employee's role with the business. These protections can include minimum wage, the right to overtime, workers' compensation,[35] unemployment benefits, and the potential for health and dental benefits if the business is large enough. An independent contractor, on the other hand, has less protections under federal law, but a lot more freedom in their relationship with the business. This distinction is also important for taxes, both for the individual and the business. A business has extra tax implications when they hire an employee, and an independent contractor is in charge of their own tax implications. So how do we the know the difference between an independent contractor and employee?

It all comes down to control, and it is all entirely fluidic. The determination between employee and independent contractor can also vary from state to state for its treatment. I will focus on federal determinations. The IRS breaks down the determination into three generalized categories: (1) *behavioral control*; (2) *financial control*; and (3) *relationship of the parties*. That said, all these laws operate on a basis of: *If it walks like a duck and talks like a duck, it is duck.* Failure to properly classify a worker as an employee can lead to issues with the IRS, as well as the employee suing the business for monies owed. Let's roam around the "You're Hired" station for some more details.

Behavioral control reflects the amount of control over the work performed by the worker—the more behavioral control, the more likely the worker is an employee. Behavioral control in this sense means indicators such as: does the person have a strict schedule, is the person told what tools they need to use for the work, is the person micromanaged or does the person receive comprehensive training. If an employer directs and exerts behavioral control over a worker, the worker is an employee, and the rights and obligations therein ensue.

Financial control reflects the financial contribution and control of the relationship. If the employer purchases the equipment used by the worker, that is a major indicator of an employee relationship. Additionally, an independent contractor usually pays for their own expenses and has the ability to seek out its own business enterprises. Method of payment is a big one, whereby an employee is usually paid hourly or via a yearly salary, then broken down in pay periods. An independent contractor, however, is usually hired by job or task and paid a flat fee, and thus under less financial control.

---

35 Workers' compensation refers to medical and wage benefits to workers who are injured or become ill at work.

The relationship of the parties is also considered. If the business and the worker have a contract, that can be used as evidence to determine how the relationship of the parties is categorized. But even if a contract specifically notes a worker is not an employee and is an independent contractor, the contract can be determined as not controlling the relationship of the parties if the worker does everything an employee does. Additionally, the length of the relationship of the parties is used to examine whether the individual is an employee or not. An indefinite time period may indicate employee status, whereas a limited duration often refers to an independent contractor.

We shall leave the "You're Hired" station and now continue along to the "You've Been Hired as an Employee" stop. As an employee, you are ensured some rights, these generally include a minimum wage[36] and a safe workplace. Also, your employer will be required to withhold and contribute taxes based on this relationship. There may be additional benefits if your employer has a set number of employees; such benefits may include health insurance. But there is another divergence after the "You've Been Hired as an Employee" station, that of exempt or non-exempt status, which becomes very important for items such as overtime pay.

This is, again, an *if it looks like a duck and talks like a duck, it is a duck* exercise. Exempt employees are not owed overtime for working more than 40 hours a week. At its most basic level, for a worker to be considered an exempt employee, meaning the worker is not included in the overtime rules, the worker must be paid by salary (not hourly) and must perform: (1) *executive*; (2) *administrative*; (3) *professional*; (4) *computer*; or (5) *outside sale duties*. There are general guidelines for each of these, as well. Let's take a gander.

To have an employee qualify as an executive, the employer would seek to ensure the worker has a central duty of managing the business or an important part of it, in addition to overseeing at least two employees, and they can either hire or fire those employees, or their recommendations must carry weight in that regard. To fall in the administrative role, the employee must be charged with non-manual labor that is related to managerial aspects of the business or its operational capacity. This is in addition to having some form of basic independent judgment in their role. To have the employee qualify as a professional, the employee must have a specific and advanced specialized knowledge that is acquired by either specialized instruction or specialization in a unique qualified field. Could I be more vague? Probably, but not with this next section.

As for the final two, computer and outside sales, with the advent of computer technology came the computer exemption for employees who are

---

36 There is a base wage that employers must pay their employees.

a computer systems analyst, computer programmer, software engineer, or other similarly skilled computer worker. Last but not least, is the outside sales representative. Often called offsite sales reps, these individuals are ones that drive sales by working in the field and visiting customers. It is through the use of these five employment categories that, if structured correctly, an employer can avoid paying overtime. It does not end there, though; in addition to all these categories, there are some very specific jobs that qualify as exempt.

Those specific exempt jobs include employees of railroads, domestic services workers that live in the employer's residence, and employees of motion picture theaters. This last one interested me, so I did some research. According to the *Hollywood Reporter*, "The rationale for the exemption at the time was that theaters could not afford the labor costs because of low profit margins, poor box office, and rising costs." Coupled with the lack of overtime, theater employees were also not eligible for minimum wage, but as the *Reporter* continues, "[w]hile the minimum-wage exemption was removed in 1974, the overtime exemption has remained, to the puzzlement of labor experts." Pretty strange, right?

All the various nuances of exempt versus non-exempt are usually taken into consideration in determining an employee's status. For example, is the person really a professional or not? Do they oversee people but lack the ability to recommend firing them? This balancing act is similar to the differentiation between employer and independent contractor. Both of these differentiations can sometimes find themselves being litigated before a court where an employee claims they should have been non-exempt and thus entitled to overtime pay (time and a half).

> **eXperimental Tip:** Hey, don't I get overtime for all this? Determining whether someone is an employee vs. an independent contractor or non-exempt vs. exempt is a fun and useful exercise. The reality of it is most full-time, hourly workers should be classified as non-exempt employees. There are so many fun items to work through—does the worker set their own hours? What if they set their own hours but the supplies are given to them by the employer? Is the outside sales rep an independent contractor or an exempt employee? Working through issues such as this is a great way to explore the early stops along the employment train route.

We have seen variances and how they work for the business and the individual's benefit. This section, again, is just covering the basics of federal law, as state laws vary and change in more frequency. The basics of this are important from a business planning ideal. I am going to take us on a new side route up a mountain pass. The first being stop being "You are an Authorized Immigrant Worker" station, essentially non-United States citizens who are authorized to work. Choo choo!

At the "You are an Authorized Immigrant Worker" station, we learn about the two main types of foreign workers. A business may only hire a non-United States citizen who has been granted the right to legally work in the United States by the federal government. There are two types of non-United States citizens who are authorized to work, lawful permanent residents[37] and select non-residents. A lawful permanent resident is the proper title for an individual who has been approved to reside in the United States on a permanent basis; they are more commonly known as a Green Card holder, the Green Card being the proof of their new resident status. Fun fact, the Green Card is no longer green; it obtained its name from the 1940s to the 1960s when the card was a vibrant green. Lawful permanent residents are usually not limited on who their employer is and can enter the job market just as a United States citizen would. Non-immigrants are a little different and that is where we will be heading on our next stop, "Non-Immigrant Junction."

At "Non-Immigrant Junction" station, we are introduced to the wide variety of visas that allow for a foreign national to enter the United States and work here. Non-immigrants authorized to work in the United States usually have to be petitioned by a specific employer to fill a specific position. These jobs can range from the complex, requiring college level or higher degrees, to the physically rigorous such as agricultural workers. Non-immigrant workers also can include crewmembers on cargo or cruise ships and even registered nurses working in hospitals. Non-immigrants are hired for a set period of time, and thus are considered to be temporary workers.[38] The general idea is that there is a gap in the labor market here in the United States and the business must look beyond the market to bring a worker from abroad, as there is no one local who can perform such a function. Non-immigrant visas are signified by lettering, for example the H-visas[39] or D-visas[40] and usually

---

37 There is a caveat here, as some applications to become a lawful permanent resident allow the individual to obtain a work permit during their time waiting for their application. Additionally, applications like asylum, Violence Against Women Act petitions, and visas related to assisting law enforcement come with the ability to file for a work permit.
38 Some non-immigrants can make the transfer over to lawful permanent residents, but the track for that can be extensive.
39 H-visas represent the family of generalized "Temporary Worker" visas, such as H-1B, which is a specialty occupation visa or the H-2A for agricultural workers.
40 D-1 visa refers to longshore crewmembers.

have corresponding numbers that apply to a specific type of job, position, or role. For example, you have the E visas, which allow for individuals of certain countries that have a treaty with the United States to enter here and engage in certain roles in a business for a select period of time. Those roles are either through traders (E-1) or investors (E-2). There are also some special programs that the federal government has established as a means of training foreign workers or opening up the ability to bring over a person for both employment and language and cultural exchanges in the United States. These positions fall under two visa categories: (1) the J-Visa Exchange Visitor Program, which is a cultural exchange program that focuses in part on au pair, medical, business, or research experiences, and (2) the Q-visa, commonly known as the Disney Visa. We are going to stop at the "J-1 Exchange" station and walk around to explore the view.

We begin our tour at the "J-1 Exchange" station by looking at the history of the J visa. The J visa's origins go back to 1961, and the creation of the Mutual Educational and Cultural Exchange Act. This Act was created by Senator J. William Fulbright[41] with the purpose to increase the understanding of American culture by inviting over select individuals to learn about America. The Act harmonized previous similar immigration allowances fashioned over two decades preceding it. The Act did so with an eye towards the Cold War. As Professor Kit Johnson notes, the federal government "saw in the Act the potential for drawing members of the international community into a pro-American, and thus anti-communist, stance by means of education and cultural exchange."

Currently, the United States Citizenship and Immigration Services notes that the J-1 visa is authorized for foreign individuals to participate in a set of approved programs for the purpose of teaching, instructing or lecturing, studying, observing, conducting research, consulting, demonstrating special skills, receiving training, or to receive graduate medical education or training. The federal government designates which entities can act as exchange sponsors. These federally sanctioned programs are designed to promote the interchange of persons, knowledge, and skills in the fields of education, arts, and science. Examples of exchange visitors under the J-1 visa include but are not limited to: (1) professors or scholars; (2) research assistants; (3) students; (4) trainees; (5) teachers; (6) specialists; (7) au pairs; and (8) camp counselors.

---

41 You may recognize the last name. Senator Fulbright created the Fulbright scholarship program, formed in 1946; it is one of the most recognized scholarship programs. In the senator's own words, "The Fulbright Program's mission is to bring a little more knowledge, a little more reason, and a little more compassion into world affairs and thereby increase the chance that nations will learn at last to live in peace and friendship." By all means, take some time to learn a little bit more about the former senator from Arkansas.

Many J visa beneficiaries must return home for a period of two years with the idea to spread the knowledge they gained and hopefully say nice things about America. The J-1 visa is varied but tied to the spread of American ideals.

The Q-visa, on the other hand, is a marvel of its age and reminds us of just how far Disney is willing to go to get exactly what they need. It is also a fantastic way to end our train ride and move back into retroventurism. Thus, we have reached our final destination. We disembark in 1982 at the Walt Disney World Resort. Before us lies EPCOT Center.

CHAPTER 10
Employees of Tomorrow, Today: Part 2: Putting Retro into Retroventurism

On October 1, 1982, a variation of Walt's Experimental Prototype Community of Tomorrow opened in the Walt Disney World Resort and was named EPCOT Center. As educator and researcher Alan Bowers notes, Walt's EPCOT "had been discussed, dissected, examined, delayed, teased, and reconfigured multiple times in the fifteen years since Walt Disney's death." The version that stands before us (well, the us that is traveling back in time on a magical employment train) is markedly different than what Walt had left as his living blueprint.

The completed EPCOT Center, a planned environment to its core, was actually the combination of two early ideas for what to do with Walt's vision. One portion was Future World, a theme park dedicated toward the future and exploration of the world around us and what it could be. Future World would be filled with areas, attractions, and rides with such inspirational names as, Spaceship Earth, Living Seas, the Land, Journey into Imagination, Communicore, Universe of Energy, the World of Motion, and Horizons. Sticking to the tradeshow element of Walt's original vision, each attraction came with either semi-permanent or rotating corporate sponsors.

While EPCOT Center's promotional material from that time referred to it as a community, it was not a city but a true planned environment. It was still noticeably different than Magic Kingdom's Tomorrowland, which was geared much more towards fantasy attractions and relied on existing Disney intellectual property. The original Future Land was aimed more at edutainment, lacking a reliance on Disney fantasy. "Edutainment" is a word used by Walt himself to discuss the combination of the intent to educate utilizing entertainment. EPCOT Center was the shining gem of this ethos. As EPCOT Center's dedication plaque notes, "May EPCOT Center entertain, inform and inspire. And above all, may it instill a new sense of belief and pride in man's ability to shape a world that offers hope to people everywhere." Future Land was only half of the figure eight that makes up EPCOT Center.

The top half of the park is the World Showcase, which seems to find its origins in Walt's original shopping district in EPCOT. The World Showcase is a ring circling a lake of various foreign themed buildings and exhibits, some containing rides or attractions, each one of them with food to eat, beverages to drink, and stores in which to shop. The countries that would eventually be represented along the lake are Mexico, Norway, China, Germany, Italy, the United States, Japan, Morocco, France, the United Kingdom, and Canada. While Walt's EPCOT, with its themed shopping district, was meant to be under a dome, more akin to a luxury enclosed shopping center, the World Showcase does get remarkably close to Walt's original plan. Even more so, the Disney Cast Members that work at each of the country pavilions are mainly residents of those countries. As Bowers notes, the foreign Cast Members "are really there to play a part; in this instance, they add a bit of 'reality' and legitimacy to the synthetic environment."

> eXperimental Tip: Brings me back to the xofa! Yes, the xofa again. Alan Bowers is the one that clued me into the idea of Walt's EPCOT having the residents intermingle with guests, discussing the xofa. As mentioned, I personally believe Walt's EPCOT was to be a contrivance, a show, and the residents would serve a similar function to the foreign Cast Members in EPCOT by bringing a bit of "reality" and "legitimacy" to the planned environment. As Bowers continues, "When one overhears French being spoken between co-workers in the France pavilion, it can be pleasantly disorienting." The same could be said of the overhearing the amazing folding convenience of the xofa; a guest would be transported into the Community of Tomorrow, not merely passing through, but amongst it. Bowers's studies revealed that, "the disorientation and skewing of reality is, paradoxically, one of the most alluring characteristics to the Disney parks." The same would have been said about Walt's EPCOT. This feeling is captured in the 2015 Disney motion picture movie Tomorrowland. The scene I am referring to is the Tomorrowland pin scene with the main character, Casey. In that scene, Casey is transported to a living blueprint of a Tomorrowland that looks very similar to Progress City. I will not give anything away, but this eXperimetal Tip is to encourage you to watch the movie and see if you can grasp a connection between Casey's journey using the Tomorrowland pin and Bowers's "pleasantly disorienting" comment above.

It is to the early foreign Cast Members at EPCOT Center that we now turn in order to discuss the Q-visa. From the start, Disney wanted the World Showcase to be fully staffed by individuals from the countries represented in the pavilions, and so it was. Initially, when we visit the early version of the World Showcase, the foreign Cast Members are not using the Q-visa, they are actually using J-1 visas. However, as time progresses, the federal government begins to become wary of abuse of the J-1 visa and its use by companies like Disney, which, granted, seems warranted—for example, Disney was bringing over German individuals to work with other Germans in a recreated Germany, that does not seem focused on the spread of American ideals back to Germany, now does it? As the 1990s loomed ahead, so did the potential for the federal government to stop or modify the J-1 visa. A Walt Disney World executive named Duncan Dickson took the reins to direct Disney to a brand new immigration frontier.

Professor Kit Johnson covers the lobbying and history of the Q-visa across two law review articles. The short of it is Dickson had a choice between fighting to save the J-1 visa or go a new route and ask for new legislation to be enacted. Sound familiar? Roy Disney would be proud. Except as opposed to the creation of the Improvement District on the state level, immigration is controlled on the federal level. It was to U.S. Congress Dickson had to turn, utilizing U.S. Representatives, especially their aides, to help draft legislation for the creation of a new visa. Like Roy before him, Duncan succeeded. Johnson notes that, "It was a remarkable insight. Dickson was not a lawyer. Yet he saw what even experienced lawyers sometimes fail to recognize: If the law does not help you, perhaps the law itself can be changed." As we have seen, this was part and parcel of the Disney ethos; laws are made by people and they can be changed by people, and no one knows people better than Disney company.

The Q-visa was ultimately crafted for an international cultural exchange program in which the foreign worker would, as part of the worker's employment, share the history, culture, and traditions of the worker's country. As the United States Citizenship and Immigration Services states, "[t]he Q cultural exchange program is for the purpose of providing practical training and employment, and sharing the history, culture, and traditions of your home country with the United States." It was perfectly built for Disney to create the immersive atmosphere of the World Showcase the architects of the park wanted. The stage has been set and the cast could now arrive.

So is an employee by any other name just an employee? I want to take some time in this employment law chapter to get to know Disney employees. The reason I want to do this is because we are going to end this chapter by engaging in theoretical retroventurism by imagining who exactly would live and work in Walt's EPCOT. But to learn about imaginary people I am going to make up that live in a place that does not exist, I first think it is best to talk to two real life Disney Cast Members. So pull a up chair—I want to you to meet Rosamund and Vander.

Richard: Rosamund and Vander, thank you so much for taking the time to sit and talk with my friend [don't be shy, tell them your name] and me. I told my friend here that you both would be willing to give us some insights on what it means to be a Cast Member. Rosamund or Vander can I offer you anything to drink? No? You sure? I bet our host has something in the cabinet [I nudge you]. Nope, nobody wants anything? Well, I could go for a smoked bishop [you should now imagine our interview taking place near a fire and it is cold outside]. Well, let us get started while our host prepares my drink. To the beginning then, what was it like to be interviewed to work at Walt Disney World?

Rosamund: When I applied to work for Disney, you would apply in person at the Casting Center, a beautiful and whimsically Disney building where you are greeted by the door from Alice in Wonderland and make your way up a character-filled up ramp to the main floor. I watched an "Introduction to working at Walt Disney World' that focused on guest service, the essence of being a Cast Member, and what the next steps would look like. A recruiter and I talked about what I would want to do. About fifteen minutes or so into the conversation, she asked if I would be interested in a "new team," and we went over some role requirements. About a week after that, I began my journey as a Cast Member.

Vander: Disney is very aware and proud of its origin and history. The story of its founder, Walt Disney, is something that is not only preserved but also passed down to every new member of his company through its orientation course, "Traditions." I believe that this course is one of the first exposures you receive as a Cast Member that sets this company apart from any other. The fact that we take the time to share the founding of our company through the story of Walt, his trials, his defeats, and ultimately successes, leading to the creation of stories and characters that we have come to know and love to this day, is what helps build the initial investment into your new role and its common goal.

Richard: That is amazing, the focus on being oriented towards guests from day one and the reinforcement of Walt's history, and the traditions behind being a Cast Member is quite unique to Disney. I like the use of the word whimsical by Rosamund, and Vander hits on an interesting point when he notes that "investment" one has with the company from early on. What about the idea of being a Cast Member as opposed to an employee, is a rose still a rose if it goes by another name?

Rosamund: So, there are lots of things that make us part of the general "employee population of theme parks and resorts." The thing about being a Cast Member is that everything is a little more magical. We have special nomenclature and everyday jargon for things (i.e. employees termed as Cast Members, uniforms termed as costume, work location termed as onstage/backstage… and the list goes on), our communication (both internal and external) is filled with bright characters and colors. What stands out to me the most is that our "work life" really is a reflection of our brand and you learn very quickly if the values and "Cast Member lifestyle" is right for you. In general, the positive and optimistic attitudes that we see in Disney films and the image we project to our guests onstage really is the overall 'feel' of being a Cast Member. As a Cast Member, I feel valued and respected by my team, executive leadership, and the decisions made by those all the way at the top who I may never interact with personally but know we are all in this together. I also feel empowered to do some pretty great things for our guests in the name of guest service and "doing the right thing"… A foundational idea that is almost omnipresent in everything we do.

Vander: To the same regard, it's the feeling of connection and investment in our company's brand and product (i.e. our stories and characters) that make employment at the Walt Disney company different from any other. Not many companies give you the opportunity to sell abstract emotions and lifetime memories as its goal. So it's the fact that we get to "work" at a place built to resemble fantasy worlds, painted in bright colors, with unique storylines and lined with characters that you already know and love, topping it all off with the ability to welcome guests into this world with you that make this a special place to work and what keeps us coming back for more.

Richard: Rosamund and Vander, you both really get to the heart of what being a Cast Member means; we can see the use of specific nomenclature to help create the feel. But really as Rosamund aptly notes, it's the ability to "project" what Vander eloquently calls "abstract emotions" towards guests that may really be the differentiation between your standard employee and a Cast Member. You both comment on the connection and togetherness Cast Members feel not only with company executives but the brand and products as well. Wow! Now what about actually working on Walt Disney World property, how does it make you feel? Be honest.

Rosamund: As I'm sure many Cast Members will say when asked this question, working on property is, for the most part…again, no one is perfect…. magical. In many cases, to get to work we walk through the same locations our guests save up for years, in some cases, to visit again and again; sometimes guests are only able to visit once… and all I can think is "Wow, I get to see this every day… I get to be PART of this every day!" There are lots of events and special moments we get to witness (engagements, family gatherings, and sometimes even difficult moments) that an employee of another company would not. We are in the business of "creating happiness," and it's not just for guests… for Cast too.

Vander: Walt Disney World has been able to achieve its namesake's goal, a "world" filled with unique properties all themed differently. The ability to escape to these different areas all within a fifteen-minute drive from each other is incredible. Personally, I love being able to go to a resort that's themed after the Pacific Northwest or Polynesian Islands and then being able to walk around the world and visit different cultures at one of its parks.

Richard: The atmosphere appears to be key. As Rosamund notes, Disney is in the business of "creating happiness" for its Cast Members as well. Vander reflects that in his draw toward the various themed areas of the resorts.

Vander: I also want to add that the Walt Disney Company is constantly expanding its reach and providing its guests with new and unique experiences. One of my favorite things about our company is its trajectory while keeping in mind where we came from. The fact that we started with one man, his ideas, and having faced many challenges that could have defeated him yet he persisted and was able to create movies and a theme park, and that we have been able to expand on those ideas and create new ones is fantastic. I always wonder what Walt Disney would think of his world today.

Richard: Vander, you really capture an interesting aspect of the Disney company, the desire for what is next. This is connected to Walt's desire never to rest on his laurels. To answer your question, I think Walt would look at the Disney company today and say, "Great! But on to tomorrow!" Thank you two so much. I see our host was so enthralled that I never received my smoked bishop. Well, maybe next chapter.

So there we have it. This discussion with Rosamund and Vander gives us an idea of what a Cast Member can mean and, more specifically, how Cast Members feel about their roles with the Disney Company, specifically those that work at Walt Disney World Resort. It is an interesting note on the current employment structure of Disney.[42] Rosamund and Vander also give us a glimpse as to the ways Disney cultivates their Cast Member ethos. Rosamund and Vander are both U.S. Citizens, but there may be additional advantages of Disney bringing foreign workers or exchange visitors to share in

---

42 At the time I am writing this, Disney may be forced to use non-foreign employees at its World Showcase due to the coronavirus and ensuing restrictions that followed.

this ethos.

Foreign workers may be exempt from some employment taxes. They also tend to live in housing owned by Disney or operated by a third party affiliate, which is an additional financial element for Disney. The big one, however, is continuity, as a foreign worker is only allowed to remain in the United States if they are working for their sponsor. Johnson notes this makes foreign workers "more dependable employees." But it is to the living arrangements I now want to turn, as it will bring us one step closer to our retroventurism goal.

Disney maintains several apartment complexes for its exchange visitors under either the J-1 or Q visa. These apartment complexes were built on land that used to be a part of the Reedy Creek Improvement District, but subsequent to either their repurposing for exchange visitor use or construction, the land upon which they sit was de-annexed. De-annexing is a process by which Disney releases areas of land back to the county, either Osceola or Orange, meaning the land is no longer located in the Reedy Creek Improvement District. Regardless of the de-annexing, Disney either owns or leases the apartment complexes; however, with the complexes being off Improvement District property, Disney does not exercise its full allotment of control. Although it establishes rules for its residents.

eXperimental Tip: So foreign employees don't actually live at Disney World? Maybe you can help me and publish your findings so I can one day find them. It is unclear why Disney de-annexes the land under the apartment complexes. It appears they are solely used for the housing of foreign workers. My presumption is the de-annexation occurs to avoid the voting issues that arose after Avery that affords residents voting rights in municipalities. I have researched this element and it appears temporary non-immigrants are not entitled to vote in municipal elections, unless a city has allowed them to. Disney's main concern, as was discussed with the Avery decision, was individuals gaining the right to vote even if they did not own land. Foreign workers presumably would not impact this voting issues and Disney would remain in control. So why de-annex? Why take the land out of the Reedy Creek Improvement District and give it back to Orange and Osceola County? I did read the de-annexation of the land was as a favor for the counties, for the counties would gain tax revenue from the development. This is reported by Geri Throne in a 1986 Orlando Sentinel article, "Disney De-Annexation Means Fees for Orange." Geri reports, "County officials were worried last fall that Disney would build the apartments in Reedy Creek and then de-annex them to the county, thus avoiding county impact fees and regulation [worth over a quarter of a million dollars]. Disney is motivated to de-annex residential development because it does not want to add new voters to Reedy Creek." As mentioned, I find this interesting if the complexes were only to be used for exchange visitors. I found specifics for at least three of the complexes that were de-annexed. Vista Way, a 462-unit apartment complex was developed and is owned directly by Disney on land formerly within the Improvement District but was de-annexed in 1990. Chatham Square, a 448-unit apartment complex, and The Commons, a 280-unit apartment complex, were developed and are owned by a third party and leased to Disney on land formerly within the Improvement District in an area called the Little Lake Bryan development. Little Lake Bryan was de-annexed in 1993. There is an additional complex called Paterson Court, and per my understanding the same above applies. Maybe you can give it a whirl, see what comes up.

Special note: A recent proposed amendment to the Florida Constitution sought to ensure that no city will never be allowed to do this either.

Disney sets the pricing for the rentals, which is considered reduced,[43] and the rent is automatically deducted from the foreign worker's paycheck. As a bonus, the rental costs include electricity, cable, waste disposal, and local phone service; additionally, there are various resort-style[44] amenities featured at each complex. One interesting aspect is there is an increased level

---

43 This is a point of contention. As per the Disney Careers website as of the writing of this book, "housing costs range from $114 to $205* (*costs subject to change) per week depending on the size of the apartment and which apartment complex a participant is assigned to live in during his or her program." Exchange visitors may be able to find cheaper room and board outside these areas, but the ease of having it all planned and picked for them is most likely appealing to many who are unfamiliar with the area.
44 That is a fun ambiguous word, is it not?

of control over the activities of the residents. A breach of the community codes could result in a termination of the exchange visitor's right to not only live in the complex but continue on the program. One such community code is regarding guests. "Guests are welcome to visit a participant's apartment complex, however overnight guests are prohibited." Disney is also extremely stringent on underage drinking at the complexes.

Interestingly enough, Disney utilizes this housing to comply with requirements under Florida law to provide affordable housing that is attributable to employment growth within the nearby area. Also, Disney has made a concerted effort toward increasing the availability of public transportation between the Improvement District and affordable housing projects elsewhere, though no monorails yet, mostly bus lines. Regardless, the idea is to alleviate concerns for exchange visitors to obtain an automobile for the duration of their stay, and Disney also is able to fulfill a government mandate by doing so. A little bit of this and a little bit of that, if you will.

We have learned the basics of employment law, heard from current Cast Members, have gotten to know how Disney obtains foreign workers for its theme parks, and how those foreign Cast Members live. What does that all mean for retroventurism? Short and simple, the residents of Walt's envisioned EPCOT were to be Disney employees, Walt had made such clear to his team. Concerning who would live in EPCOT, Walt was noted to have scratched out the words "permanent residents" in a memo from Paul Helliwell concerning EPCOT and writing in "temporary residents/tourists." Also, as one can hear in the EPCOT Film, there would be employment for all and responsibility to keep EPCOT a reality and thriving. This directly confirms Walt envisioned them to be Cast Members. Also, with the residents as Cast Members, there would be an added level of ensuring responsibility for keeping EPCOT a functioning community, however contrived. As we saw before, foreign workers are presumed to be more reliable, for they are not only getting paid, but their stay in the United States is connected to their continued employment. This is in addition to being a Cast Member, individuals who are already more loyal than your average employee, as understood per the conversation we had with Rosamund and Vander. Foreign Cast Members could be seen as a more beneficial workforce than domestic. This is even truer in Walt's EPCOT, for in addition to the possibility of them being all more reliable workers because of their immigration status, their utilization may have been an answer to the developing voting control issue that occurred with the *Avery* decision.

This is because no state has allowed non-citizens to vote in state elections since the 1920s, and while cities can allow non-citizens to vote in municipal elections, approximately only a dozen cities in the entire United States do.[45] As such, the foreign worker, as employee, may have been the magic pill to bring Walt's EPCOT into a reality. One major issue would probably have reared its head as to which visa would allow all that Walt wanted his residents to do—live, work, engage in recreation, most likely devoid of a formal educational institution connection. They could have tried the J-visa. As we know, the J-visa existed during this time, but it was not a guarantee that Disney could use the visa freely as it wanted. As such, Disney probably would have had to do what it eventually did and lobby the federal government for an EPCOT Resident Visa (or as I would like to call it for our purposes, the EPVOT, the Experimental Prototype Visa of Tomorrow).

Author Sam Gennawey does a fantastic job of taking his readers on a tour of what EPCOT would have been had it been built to Walt's specifications. It is a great portion of his book *The Promise of Progress City*, as it is pure theoretical retroventurism whereby he is taking a road map from the past and applying it, to the best of his knowledge, on what could be. One area he did not fully expound upon was what would the residents be like, and where he does, I do not fully agree with. So that is where this chapter has been steering us to. We are about to meet the residents of the Experimental Prototype Community of Tomorrow. Welcome to a parallel universe!

You and your family are traversing Walt Disney World in the monorail on the way to EPCOT. Although you are staying at a resort near Magic Kingdom, your family wants to grab a bite to eat at Sternen, the Swiss eatery located in the fully enclosed internationally themed shopping district below the Grand Emerald Disney Marquee Hotel & Resort. As such, you will be stopping at the Grand Emerald Transportation Station. Do not worry about your luggage, that is being delivered to your resort room utilizing the underground transportation systems below EPCOT.[46] You arrive to the Transportation Station just as it is coming alive.

Cast Members are already at work, baking and cooking breakfast for the many guests, just like you, arriving on the monorail or coming down from their rooms at the Grand Emerald. Residents are arriving on PeopleMovers from their homes beyond the greenbelt in EPCOT. The smells of a world bazaar waft up to you, as languages of a dozen countries mingle and fizzle below. A Cast Member greets you on the monorail exit of the Transportation Station, "Welcome to EPCOT! How may I be of assistance to you?" The Cast

45 There are ten cities in Maryland that allow this, and San Francisco allows non-citizens to vote in school board elections.
46 Disney has a similar program now where they transport guests to Walt Disney World from the Orlando airport and transport their luggage straight to their resort room. This program however may be phased out in the coming years.

Member points you in the direction of the Swiss district and you make your way down to the ground level.

Above you now, a monorail effortlessly glides by and the PeopleMover tracks continue to bring residents in, many of whom are also heading into the Swiss District. Cast Members working in the Swiss District are dressed in their Swiss-styled clothing, and you can hear the chatter of Swiss-German coming from many of the stores and restaurants you pass. As you enter the Swiss District proper, the noises from the surrounding districts seem to disappear. Replaced are soft distant sounds of a yodeler, maybe high off in some distant Swiss Alp you swear must be just around the next bend. The smell of Swiss chocolate dances up to you. A Swiss band is preparing to play, and you catch drifts of accordion being brought to life after a long night's sleep. You are fully immersed as you walk along the Swiss shops mingling with other guests and residents.

You can mark the residents by their clothing; everything seems so stylish, yet comfortably fitting. The fabric of their clothes is not like anything you've seen, for it is both form fitting and flowy. Although the residents might appear to be from different countries, they are all speaking English. Did that young woman just mention a xofa?

You settle down with your family at Sternen. A Swiss waiter brings you gipfeli and rösti, a Swiss croissant and potato pancake, and some fresh squeezed orange juice (well, you are in Florida, after all). A resident stops by your table, "Oh you ordered the gipfeli, fantastic choice! I actually just bought a Nestle gipfeli maker for my house. I love them so much. Enjoy! I came today for the fresh squeezed orange juice—it is Florida after all!" The resident leaves, and you and your family look at each other in astonishment… "Can they read minds??"

You settle into your breakfast to listen and watch the world as it moves around the eatery and the street outside. Soft yodeling echoes in. Two residents sit at a table behind you. You can hear their conversation. "Yeah I arrived yesterday from South Africa, and I am already set up at the Blue Leaf Residences."

The other resident replies, "Are you near the GreenBelt or the PeopleMover station 5?"

"Actually right in between the two, in fact this morning I just hopped on my Schwinn Votoscooter and parked it at a recharging station near the PeopleMover Station before coming in."

"Oh that's great, and I'm glad you ran into me before I returned home to Thailand next week, I can show you all the best places to eat."

"Thank you, I heard we are getting Tesla jetpacks to try out in the

Industrial Park soon."

"Yep, in two weeks, just in time for me to not be here anymore, but I've already lined up my return next year."

"Oh, that's great. I've got a few days until I start at It's a Small World ride at Magic Kingdom."

"Perfect, we do have time to explore. Let's meet up at the Tiki Bar at Green Leaf Estates, say around 5pm. I still need to finish my product reviews for this last month so I can hand them back the New Products Coordinator." Your concentration fades away as an accordion begins to play outside...

There we have it, our guided tour of the EPCOT residents comes to a close. The residents of EPCOT would have been Cast Members, and not just any Cast Members, they would have been foreign workers eligible to live and work in EPCOT under a newly created non-immigrant visa called the EPVOT. As you could probably see, the Cast Members in their "residents" role were to engage guests and talk about their travel and living arrangements, specifically naming products they were entrusted with testing. This all most likely would have been instructed to them by a Disney Cast Member training after going through their "Traditions" training. This forced engagement of guests at random is nothing controversial; many clothing retailers instruct their staff to complement shoppers on a specific item of clothing they have on in order to create a warm atmosphere and increase sales.

In fact, the residents would not even have been in the international shopping districts by chance, they would actually be working, but as a resident as opposed to, say, a waiter. As such, many Cast Members may have had two jobs, half the work week spent, for example, serving tapas in the Spain District, the other half walking around the China District as a resident grabbing lunch.[47] All this would be done to fully immerse guests into the EPCOT experience. To create that pleasantly disorienting atmosphere Bowers discusses. Why would a worker agree to do this, to be a part of a contrivance?

As we saw with Rosamund and Vander, there is an ethos that comes with being a Cast Member. Something beyond an employee, and being actively *invested* in something as *whimsical* and ambitious as Walt's EPCOT would most likely have galvanized a worker's interest in keeping up the contrivance. Additionally, as Johnson noted, foreign workers make for more eager employees, as their status here in the United States is linked with being sponsored as an employee. So there is an added layer beyond the Disney magic to ensure compliance with their Cast Member training.

47 Disney would need to be careful about having the Cast Member "be on" all the time, as that may actually lead to issues with overtime. So there could be many alternatives to this; some Cast Members may just have jobs as residents, but I believe having more diversified resident/service roles for more Cast Members would create a better employee atmosphere.

The Cast Members would have lived in both the apartments and the residential areas of EPCOT, as there would be some hierarchy, no doubt, as to the living arrangements. Cast Members in higher positions, supervisors and researchers at the industrial zone, would most likely have been afforded housing in the low-density housing, and Cast Members in service-oriented positions may have been located in the apartment complexes, which would still be conveniently located to nightclubs and other entertainment areas in the internationally themed shopping district. Additionally, one could imagine that Disney would de-annex land and build a low-density satellite community for some of their industrial partners' employees to live. These employees could be lab technicians, engineers, craftspeople, designers, and product developers that would work at the industrial park near EPCOT. These non-Disney associated employees could have their families with them, as living in de-annexed land they would not impact voting rights. It could also be that any young non-school age children could attend daycare at EPCOT, adding to a level of family orientation in the community.

The residents of EPCOT would predominantly be young and single, as Disney would most likely only admit the actual Cast Member to reside at EPCOT. In theory, Disney could allow foreign-born spouses to join the Cast Members but would need to prohibit American-born spouses. The concern being if American spouses were admitted, there could be issues raised with voting rights. Any prohibition of American spouses may have been an issue, resulting in inverse discrimination based on nationality. As such, spouses or significant others would most likely be prohibited across the board. However, they could possibly admit children regardless of nationality under the age of 18, as they would lack voting rights. But Disney would most likely want their Cast Members focused on EPCOT. Just as with current foreign-based workers and students that take part in the Disney exchange visitors programs, this situation is more fitted towards younger individuals.

As for the living arrangements, Cast Members would have probably been under the same rules as those exchange visitors are in the apartment complexes utilized by Disney now: no underage drinking, no overnight guests. With all those young, single employees, the overnight guest issue would have been an interesting issue over the years.[48] Regardless, the foreign

48 Johnson notes in her work that many exchange visitors come to the Disney program hearing that apartment complexes are a place to party and to "get laid." The reality of these places being a combination of a college dorm and an Olympic village is probably not unfounded. A 2018 Instyle magazine article on the Olympic Village looks for insight into the athlete hookup culture that's so widely reported. An Olympian interviewed notes, "What happens in the village, stays in the village," continuing she says, "That rumor may have some validity." I do not mention this to be salacious, but to acknowledge the reality of inviting 20,000 strangers picked to live together under one roof. I mean, even more exciting is the reality of a child being born, a child of Tomorrow. In the

Cast Members would be here under the EPVOT, and thus a temporary period, most likely nine months to maybe even 16 months, depending on the job they were filling. As we saw in our theoretical roleplaying retroventurism journey, English would have been required to be spoken when they were in their roles as residents, but at home and in work their native language would be encouraged.

At home, the residents would be fulfilling their dual purpose, that as product testers of American ingenuity. If prototype products—yes, the xofa—were being developed in the industrial park, they would be delivered to the low-density homes and apartments of the Cast Members to try out. They would need to relay reports on the product viability to designated New Product Coordinators. Again, this may seem forced, but in reality that is the novelty of tradeshow and concept car shows—looking is one thing, but what about actually using it? Additionally, all the Cast Members would return to their home countries with not just ancillary knowledge of American ingenuity but firsthand physical knowledge.[49] Disney's corporate partners would also get an open and available test group for their latest products. It really is an amazing relationship.

One interesting aspect that would need to be managed is guests visiting the apartments, business offices, low-density houses, and greenbelt. There would have needed to be some form of guided tours, as Cast Members could not be forced to "be on" 24/7 in violation of U.S. and state labor laws, in addition to any overtime issues. As such, Disney would need to create certain areas managed almost as a *Truman Show*[50] atmosphere in the outer rings of EPCOT. This would be necessary, as opposed to letting the guests wander the community fully and visit any house. Guided tours would have been led to houses to meet "random" residents and discussions would be had about latest products and services they are utilizing.

Outside of the guided tours, Cast Members would need to be aware that they would be visible to guests who would be traveling overhead on the monorail or PeopleMovers, or walking amongst them in a green belt. As such, there would be heightened rules and restrictions for the residents' activities. They were not truly normal residents taking part in their daily activities, but pieces on stage. Disney would need to take this into consideration when addressing the mental health of the Cast Members.

---

words of Jeff Goldblum, "Life finds a way."

49 No doubt Cast Members would need to sign confidentiality and non-disclosure agreements, promising not to disclose the inner workings of the new products.

50 *The Truman Show* is a 1998 Motion Picture starring Jim Carrey as the titular character Truman who grows up in a presumed picture-perfect community, which actually turns out to be a television studio lot of which he is ultimately unaware.

In fact, I would wager there would need to be not just training, but mental health experts and holistic helpers on hand. I would perceive numerous holistic groups would be planning activities for the Cast Members throughout their stay, such as exercise clubs, book clubs, yoga courses, laughter as medicine clinics, etc. to allow them to alleviate the stress of the heightened restrictions on personal freedoms. This may seem odd, but one must imagine how astronauts are treated and/or individuals picked to live in biodomes; this is a similar process, but on a much larger, more ambitious scale. Beyond EPCOT, Cast Members, just as current exchange visitors, would have been able to take some breaks to explore greater Florida and the United States.

At the end of the day though, these foreign workers' main mission was to be a Cast Member of EPCOT and to live up to the ideal that Walt's EPCOT tried to capture, and most likely many would take pride in this. Being *invested* in something greater than them, *serving* a role for the future of technology, *showing* guests how wonderful the Community of Tomorrow could really be. Hopefully you enjoyed a taste of theoretical retroventurism. But let's you and I jump back into reality again for a chapter. Shall we dare? I want to take you on a journey to two towns the Walt Disney company did build in Florida. So pack your bags, we are going to Celebration!

CHAPTER 11
The Real Estate of Affairs

Disney did, in a fashion, keep its word about bringing residents to Walt Disney World. I say "in a fashion" for reasons we will learn in this chapter. The crux is the Disney company has built two communities in Florida—the town of Celebration and the newly developing community of Golden Oak. These areas, as of the writing of this book, are fundamentally different, with Golden Oak being more residential-focused and Celebration being a functioning town. They do share much in their basic development. Discussing these two also allows us to talk about real estate law, especially in the realm of the commercial aspects.

Real estate law is a topic often found in business law classes or as a separate adjoining course. Real estate law, in the business law context, generally refers to commercial real estate law, which regulates the transactional elements of the purchase and sale of land and/or buildings for business use, but it also covers other items, such as leases, condominium and community housing law, zoning, and land use.

A standard course on commercial real estate focuses on purchase and sale agreements as well as lease agreements. As far as leases, that means it also delves into a separate, but connected, area of the law, which is landlord tenant law. Landlord tenant law is a highly regulated area of contract law because it is often affecting residential housing, thus governments tend to take an extra look at landlord tenant law. This law varies from state to state, with some states favoring landlords and others favoring tenants. This is true both in the residential and commercial sense. In the commercial context, when one speaks of leases it is over land, a building, or a unit inside a building.

Purchase and sale agreements cover the transfer of title (another word for ownership) of the property from one party to another. The purchase and sale agreement is a contract. The document evidencing the sale, or showing that title has been transferred, is called a deed. A deed should be registered with the county where the land is sold, so it may be recorded in the official books of the county. This is to ensure a clean title when future transfers are made. There are different types of deeds based upon the nature of the transaction. Some of these differences can have lasting impacts of the type of title given and how the land may be transferred in the future. For example, quit claim deeds, which transfer whatever title an owner may have, are common at the end of divorce proceedings whereby one ex-spouse gives over any ownership he or she may have had in a property. You and I previously discussed commercial real estate transactions when looking at all the moves Walt used to wrangle all the property he wanted in Florida.

Condominium and community housing law focuses on residential property, though I find it important to mention in the business context, as this type of law plays a special role in both the town of Celebration and the Golden Oak community. This area of the law, which is also controlled by statutes in some states, concerns how the private associations that govern condominiums and some residential communities act. Homeowners' associations fall under statutory standards for their operation and governance. A homeowners' association is a private organization in a community that makes and enforces rules for the properties in that community and the residents that live therein. People who purchase property in such a community automatically become members of the homeowners' association and are required to pay dues. As you can imagine, there are some homeowners' associations that can be extremely restrictive about what residents can do with their own properties. Statutes are also in play with the aim to focus dispute resolution between the association and its residents, or just between the residents themselves when those may arise.

> eXperimental Tip: Ah, homeowners' association; some people love them, with their forced rules and uniformity, and others can't stand the idea of living under such rules and paying costs that may seem frivolous. Associations control aspects such as lawn and exterior house maintenance, regulations on vehicles, exterior paint colors, and extra structures such as tool sheds or pools. By use of fines and other means, the association can control the residents in the community. Some of these items reflect more uniformity concerns, such as paint colors and extra structures, as opposed to property value concerns such as lawn and exterior house maintenance. Additionally, some associations can issue special financial levies against residents to fix community elements, build guardhouses, and other similar items. Some individuals may seek to live outside a homeowners' association to avoid these restrictions and potential costs. For those who live in a city, some of these care items fall under the City Code and Ordinances. These ordinances may make

116

a person feel like they are living in an association, for they require similar things such as lawn care or trash removal, for example. Cities do this to ensure property values are maintained. Which side of the fence are you on, homeowners' association or no? And why? Is it the added levels of control that bother you, or are there other reasons? It is a fun exercise to ferret out for yourself, as well as in a group setting.

The last area of real estate law I want to touch on is land use and zoning. Land use law focuses on the legal and regulatory issues that can pop up during the development, and later use, of land. It covers the processes by which landowners and developers must adhere in order to obtain government approval for a project. The potential hurdles include applying for revisions to comprehensive plans, re-zonings, development orders, special use permits, variances, subdivision approvals, and development agreements, and that is just a basic list. So we can start to see why Walt wanted to avoid land use regulations for fear of overburdening his project. At its heart, land use law is the means in which a government regulates land development, and includes special focuses on historic, cultural, and natural resources. Zoning and urban planning fall under land use as well, as governments seek to maximize public resources through zoning while also maintain property value in order to generate taxes.

This covers the basics of real estate law and the ways it can intertwine with business. It is important to note that it is one of the few topics in this text that actually has a large impact outside of business, as real estate law also covers a vast amount of non-commercial regulations and laws. But it is that combination of commercial and residential that actually leads us into our connection with the two Disney developed properties, Celebration and Golden Oak. In addition, we are going to check out Disney's operations in Paris and revisit our old friend Opa-locka, but first let's celebrate in Celebration!

Celebration, Florida is a community built by the Disney company directly adjoining the Reedy Creek Improvement District. The Celebration community was developed with the core functions of "building a better place and a better way to live." As Celebration currently describes the path of its origins, "in order to draft a blueprint for fulfilling such a vision and oversee its creation, the Walt Disney Company founded The Celebration Company." Notice that "blueprint" language, an interesting word choice similar to Walt's "living blueprint" in the EPCOT Film.

In aiming to build a better place, the Celebration Company formulated five ideals that would guide every aspect of the community's creation. These ideals would intertwine with the way the residents would live and interact with their community. The five guiding ideals are known as the Celebration Cornerstones, and they consist of: (1) *sense of community*; (2) *sense of place*; (3) *focus on technology*; (4) *focus on education*; and (5) *focus of health*.

The plan for Celebration as a residential community was born in the late 1980s. During this time period, Michael Eisner was the CEO of the Disney company. Upon the official announcement of the project, Eisner stated that the building of the town was, in essence, "to make good on Walt's unrealized dream for a city of the future." But the reality became slightly different. As Peter Rummell, one of Disney's lead team members on the development of the Celebration property, reported to Eisner, "It will have fiber optics and Smart Houses, but the feel will be closer to Main Street than to Future World." Thus while the community of Celebration, with its five ideals, had the contextual feel of Walt's EPCOT—it was even envisioned for 20,000 permanent residents—the end result would on its face, and in most aspects, appear different.

The residences of Celebration range from manor and estate homes to townhomes and apartments. The styles of the residences are Classical, Colonial, French, Coastal, Mediterranean, and Victorian. Most manor and estate homes have a front porch that faces the street and access to rear garages for cars through service alleys. The community includes a sizeable greenbelt and public amenities such as a golf course and nature trails. Celebration includes a state-of-the-art hospital and medical campus. There is also a town center, which includes the standard affair of a town hall, post office, bank, cinema, retail, office space, and a hotel. Apartments were built above the retail sections in the town center.

Celebration's design was intended to be a place to live, play, and work. Celebration has an office park near the community, a sort of nod to the industrial park idea that was in Walt's EPCOT vision. The office park, Celebration Place, was included early in the planning process. Different Disney divisions occupy much of that office park, including, for example, the headquarters for Disney Cruise Line. The Reedy Creek Improvement District's administration arm maintains a connection in the community as well through the provision of some utilities. If you recall, Disney was afforded extraterritoriality for the provision of utilities dating back to the Improvement District's creation by the Florida legislature.

One element that made its way into Celebration that was excluded from the list of rights given to Roy Disney by Florida was a school.[51] A unique K-12 educational experience was developed and aimed directly at Celebration's residents. Over time, other educational institutions have been added as well, including a branch of Stetson University and a separate high school.

A drastic move came to Celebration in 2004 when Disney sold its interest in Celebration's town center to a private investor. As reporter Tarpley Hitt describes, Disney effectively sold businesses and apartments to a private firm called Lexin Capital, run by a New York City real estate developer named Metin Negrin. The apartments in the town center were subsequently turned into condominiums. Residents of the condos eventually alleged Negrin let the place fall to pieces and started bleeding the residents dry. It is reported that Negrin personally reinvested assets, collected equity, and turned a profit, all the while failing to live up to Disney's previous aggressive maintenance style for the residences. As one condo resident put it, "We find ourselves stunned awake, Rip Van Winkle-esque. Abandoned by the Disney Brand, abandoned by the Disney attorneys and their well-crafted clauses, the visible effects of neglect and mismanagement are displayed in the decay and disarray, rotting beams and mold, leaking roofs, and [the] plummeting values of our homes." According to Hitt, while Disney does still play a minimal background role in the town center, this fight has been waged between the residents and the new private investor. This goes to show what can occur when Disney exercises its rights and sells off a Disney asset and fully relinquishes control. Those who hoped for reliance on that control may be left holding the bag.[52]

> **eXperimental Tip:** Selling off select businesses and apartments is one thing, but what if Disney sold it all? Specifically, what would happen if the Disney company sold Walt Disney World Resort itself? Unthinkable, you might say. Not entirely, as it had actually been contemplated at one point (and may again after the events of the 2020 pandemic and

---

51 Richard Foglesong does a great job tracking the history of Celebration's school. Due to diminishing class sizes and over-budgeting (probably the first time anyone has ever said a school had too much money), the school became a point of contention for the community. The school itself belongs in the Osceola County School District, and eventually, to appease the county, Disney allowed for land in Celebration to be used to build a high school. This new high school would allow students outside of Celebration to attend, upsetting residents who wanted to keep their K-12 program insular.

52 As to actual residents in the Improvement District, Disney only maintains close to 50 full-time residents on the property, split amongst Lake Buena Vista and Bay Lake. These individuals are trusted Disney employees and their families, who are generally known to vote for what Disney alludes to.

the systemic losses the Disney company suffered). In 2004, Disney's theme park activities were almost purchased by the Comcast company. This raised a red flag in the hearts of the Florida legislature, as they had given so many rights to Roy all those years ago. Up to that point, though at times fractious and cumbersome, Disney had generally been a good corporate citizen to Florida. In light of the events of 2004, the Florida legislature commissioned the Office of Program Policy Analysis & Government Accountability (OPPAGA) to conduct a research report into what Florida could do if a not so "good corporate citizen" took up residence at Magic Kingdom. The report finds that there are mechanisms—federal, state, and local—in place to protect Florida if Disney did sell. There is one interesting assertion included in the report that I downright do not agree with. The report notes, "If a new entity purchased these assets, from a sound business perspective, it would need to maintain the current character of the attractions, accommodations, and other businesses within district boundaries. Any action other than maintaining these assets at the present level could have a negative effect on customer satisfaction and may dilute the business' profit level and ability to achieve an acceptable return on its investment." That I do not believe is true, for we have an example with the Celebration town center sale. It is possible to turn a profit without maintaining Disney's "aggressive maintenance style" of its assets. Any potential reliance by the Florida legislature of a new owner "maintaining these assets at the present level" is at worst foolish, and at least much more problematic than what the OPPAGA report finds. I say this, as I believe there are certain elements of Disney's aggressive standard of maintenance that may in fact be unparalleled, literally and more importantly psychologically, to the public eye. What do you think?

Before we leave Celebration, a key element you may be wondering about are the people that live there, these permanent Celebration residents. What about Disney's voting issues we talked about before? The answer lies in where the property is located. Disney de-annexed all the land that Celebration sits upon back to Osceola County. As such, Celebration, the town built by Disney, is not actually located in the Reedy Creek Improvement District but on property just outside of it.[53] In fact, they would follow the same model for their next residential endeavor, Golden Oak.

On June 23, 2010, Disney issued a press release introducing its newest residential venture, Golden Oak. "[A] one-of-a-kind luxury residential resort community offering the unprecedented opportunity to purchase a home at Walt Disney World Resort in Florida. Especially designed for resort living, Golden Oak will provide an entirely new way for families to connect with the world's best known family destination and entertainment brand." The property is located not at a distance from the theme parks like Celebration, but close to the heart of Walt Disney World Resort. It is positioned right near Disney's Fort Wilderness Campgrounds. The initial plans called for nearly 1,000 acres devoted to the project, with half of it being reserved for conservation. The community also maintains access to a Four Seasons Resort built at the same location.

I remember the first time I saw the construction of the Golden Oak residences. It took me a minute to register that they were building actual homes that close to Disney's theme parks. I had already known about Celebration, how the land for Celebration had been de-annexed. I could not believe that this land so close to the theme parks would also be de-annexed.[54] But it had been. I was able to discern this after thorough research on the internet. There is no readily available mentioning of the de-annexing by Disney press releases or websites. In fact, my break came thanks to an intrepid Disney aficionado Jack Spence and his blog post on Golden Oak from 2012 noting, "The master-plan was developed by Walt Disney Imagineering. Although Disney will maintain the day-to-day operation of the community,

---

53 As to actual residents in the Improvement District, Disney only maintains close to 50 full-time residents on the property, split amongst Lake Buena Vista and Bay Lake. These individuals are trusted Disney employees and their families, who are generally known to vote for what Disney alludes to.

54 A blog post from Michael Andrew Niel Montilla entitled "Democracy at Disneyworld, How Residents Could Affect Disney's Control Over the Reedy Creek Improvement District" also incorrectly determines the land remained on Disney/Reedy Creek property. This is an apparent error made by Reporter Michelle Stark in her *Tampa Bay Times* Piece entitled "8 facts about Walt Disney World's luxury Golden Oak neighborhood." Stark notes it's the only place where fans can own a piece of Disney property. *The Wall Street Journal* made a similar allusion, with Dawn Wotapka's piece, "Is there a Mouse in the House" where Wotapka notes, "only place in the world where you can own a home within Disney-resort boundaries." Montilla, Stark & Wotapka made an apparent error of assumption I also made prior to doing full research, that Golden Oak was still on Reedy Creek Improvement District property, or alternatively they fail to make clear the land had been de-annexed. I believe this error (or active misinterpretation) is chalked up to the proximity of Golden Oak to Disney's theme parks.

the land was de-annexed from Reedy Creek and residents will be part of Orange County." Reviewing the Orange County Property Records for some of the addresses of the residences revealed the same, indicating the property falls under Orange County.[55]

Golden Oak is, in essence, a closed residential neighborhood with access to one of the most interesting community amenities available, the Walt Disney World theme and water parks. Direct access to the parks and tickets are afforded to the residents, as well as special access to prime Disney attractions and restaurants. This of course is included as part of the homeowners' association dues, which are purportedly in the base range of $20,000 a year, with additional add-ons available. Golden Oak also includes amenities such as park areas, access for the Four Seasons Resort, and a community clubhouse. While Golden Oak is not connected to the monorail system, nor does a PeopleMover come to the neighborhood, the residents do have access to Disney's Home-to-Park shuttle services—imagine a van painted like Minnie Mouse.[56] Golden Oak's closeness to Disney's theme parks and operations in general gives us some insight into Walt's EPCOT, at least a whisper of a glimpse into the low-density residential aspects of it.

An interesting feature about the Gold Oak development is that the Disney company had predicted that community would actually fall more into the realm of a vacation home neighborhood. Disney community planners projected that 80 percent of the properties would be used as vacation homes of the rich, as opposed to actual residences of the equally rich. However, Disney started to see an uptick of families using it as their primary residences.

As to the look of the neighborhood, the residences are not themed in a sense, but feature styles, similar in nature to Celebration. The styles include Tuscan, American Farmhouse, Spanish Revival, Tudor, and Craftsman, to name a few. Golden Oak is not a town like Celebration, but is more a collection of homes. Golden Oak's ease of access to all the various elements of Walt Disney World Resort, shopping, theme parks, golf, water parks, and transportation stations gives Golden Oak a different glancing wink than, say, Celebration does to Walt's EPCOT. A wink that should not be overlooked.

There is one more Disney area I want to look at, and that is Disneyland Paris. There are some rumors, nothing official that I can find,[57] that

---

55 After finally finding the right thread to pull, I was able to locate news publications verifying the de-annexation of the land.

56 At the time I was writing this book that was the case, but I read rumors online the Minnie vans were being discontinued across the park due to factors ranging from lack of interest to low customer approval. It is unclear whether a special service will take its place just for Golden Oak residents.

57 I reached out to noted Disney historian Jim Korkis on this, and he confirmed that, while there are rumors, he has not found any concrete connection either.

Disneyland Paris and the surrounding environs owe some allegiance to Walt's EPCOT. It may be a case of correlation does not prove causation. Dating back to 2010, a contributor on Micechat (a non-official Disney forum) named Zarniwoop noted these similarities as Disneyland Paris features: (1) A "Town" of Val d'Europe that is circular (partly, at least); (2) The town is a similar size to Walt's EPCOT; (3) The main employer for the town would be Disneyland Paris; (4) There is an electric train with two stations within the circle; (5) availability of external rail and internal public transportation; (6) the existence of a shopping center with an associated village; (7) a hospital; and (8) a sizeable population. This is undoubtedly pulling at some random elements, and as mentioned, I was unable to verify that Walt's EPCOT had any impact, but it is interesting to note similarities between the two.

Now, I personally believe it is to the past that we must look to see a similar visionary city in the same vein of what Walt would propose in EPCOT. Yep, you guessed it, I am reaching back to Glenn Curtiss and Opa-locka. We are going to be doing a little bit of our own eXperimental Tip together on this one.

As a bit of refresher, 1920s Florida saw inventor, aviation and motorcycle pioneer, and at one time Fastest Man on Earth, Glenn Curtiss continue his land development project in Opa-locka after working to build the towns of Hialeah and Miami Springs. With Opa-locka, Curtiss moved to immortalize what an American Garden City really could be. By use of urban planning, Opa-locka was specifically zoned for residential, shopping, industry, and beyond sufficient leisure and green areas. Additionally, as an added Garden City and self-sustaining motif, residents were afforded their own separate garden plots to raise food.

Opa-locka was meant to be not only self-sufficient, but also self-contained with an immense number of amenities such as an airport, zoo, swimming pools, parks, golf course, fairgrounds, archery clubs, and additional garden plots. All of the structures, including its City Hall, train station, residences, and businesses were built in the Arabian Night theme; even the streets bore names from the fabled tales. Curtiss had additional themed areas in mind, Egyptian, Chinese, and English. Curtiss looked to bring in employment opportunities in manufacturing, construction, and service to heighten the self-sufficiency to its peak. Opa-locka also featured a commuter train service, one of the first in Miami at the time.

As you may recall, Opa-locka's Arabian Night thematic overtures were on full display when the rail line was officially opened. In 1927, upon the first train arrival, Opa-locka's residents and hired actors streamed forth to greet the train. In fact, an entire production and battle scene was played out before the notable visitors. Prior to the Great Depression and the death of Curtiss, construction was completed on the City Hall, train station, airport, police and fire stations, golf course, several store fronts and gas stations, apartment complexes, horse stables, residences, elementary school, and even an observation tower from which to view the burgeoning city.

Learning what we have from Walt's EPCOT, I personally have a hard time not seeing Curtiss's Opa-locka as a prototype of the Experimental Prototype Community of Tomorrow. First, I heartedly acknowledge correlation does not prove causation. There are similarities, and those similarities may rest in Walt's affinity for the Garden City model. But to me the connection goes deeper and beyond that.

We have in Opa-locka a city featuring new and fundamentally exciting modes of transportation—an airport, company buses, and a commuter train service. This foreshadows at least in part EPCOT's jetport, Disney bus lines, Minnie vans, and monorail system. The sheer amount of amenities is another element the two projects shared. Opa-locka did not have its own Magic Kingdom off in the distance, but it did have a palace for a city hall, and the robust offerings of leisure activities exceeded anything that was actually put forth by the Disney company in their own communities. One item that really strikes me is Curtiss's focus on bringing employment for the residents in the form of manufacturing, construction, and service. Almost an employment-for-all-residents mentality that was shared by Walt in his EPCOT vision. The idea of having manufacturing also directly correlates with the industrial satellite complex of Walt's EPCOT. This brings me to the last piece of the puzzle: themes.

What really drew me to making a connection between Opa-locka and Walt's EPCOT was the themed element. While the town of Celebration, and even Golden Oak, have styles, they are not themed. Themed means a place or event that has been created so that it shows a particular historical time or way of life or tells a well-known story. It is obvious that Opa-locka was a themed city, based upon Arabian Nights (telling a well-known story). What would have been equally interesting to see is what the Egyptian, Chinese, and English themes would have involved. Having a Tuscan or Colonial style home or community center does not make a theme, as such Celebration and Golden Oak both lack themeness (my word). EPCOT's theme of course was a "way of life," a Community of Tomorrow, scientific innovation with an educational outlook. Add to that the various country themed shopping districts in EPCOT.

As we saw, Opa-locka included shops themed after Arabian Nights, and its adjoining Egyptian, Chinese, and English areas would have undoubtedly as well. I should also point out the known shopping districts for Walt's EPCOT were China, Germany, Switzerland, and the United Kingdom[58] from what I have been able to locate. As such, at least two known themes were explored by both Opa-locka and EPCOT, most likely due to popularity in the American mindset but still intriguing. Unrelated to Walt's vision for EPCOT but intriguing nonetheless, in the early days of planning Walt Disney World, the Disney company meant to feature a Persian Resort. It was never built, but was to be joined by Asian, Venetian, and Polynesian resorts (the last one was constructed and exists today). Of the Persian Resort, a Disney press release imagines, "[s]tepping right out of The Arabian Nights is the Persian resort which will reign like an exotic far-Eastern palace on the Northwest shore of [Bay Lake]." It was described with "jewel-like mosques and columns [that] will rise above landscaped courtyards, while terraced sundecks offer sculpted swimming pools and 'old Persian' dining facilities." This is a reverberation of the similar type of marketing material used to encourage home buyers and visitors to Opa-locka. Truly amazing. One last fun bit is the "opening" celebrations in both Opa-locka and EPCOT Center in 1982. Both feature actors putting on a show for a list of important guests from Florida. It really is a neat element.

We are faced then with a themed Garden City in Florida, planned in the 1920s and again in the 1960s, by two innovative men. It begs the questions, why and how? I will leave that for you to explore.

A big part looking back at the designs for EPCOT and Opa-locka is the engagement of urban studies—well, technically, visionary cities studies. Visionary cities studies look at the way we want to live and how we as people reach for that goal. It focuses on how zoning, traffic, crime, and employment affect and interact with us, driving us towards something brighter. Walt Disney directly references the challenges facing cities at the time as an important role in deciding on building EPCOT.

Our leap into visionary cities studies opens up questions on urban design. Urban design is in the art of the building, the composition of the structure, and the details of the style. Planning a city is one thing, making it aesthetically connected and pleasing is quite another. This becomes even more important when your city is meant to incorporate various styles or, even greater, a centralized theme as Opa-locka and EPCOT did. Walt used

---

58 There is a question whether in an early rendering of the shopping district for EPCOT, artist Herb Ryman was depicting Ireland or the United Kingdom as a whole. The reason being on one rendering there is a bar with a distinct Irish name, but the band in front playing bagpipes are wearing traditional Scottish attire. This becomes even more interesting because the current United Kingdom Epcot Pavilion is actually featuring a theme United Kingdom from the earlier part of the twentieth century.

artists, such as Herb Ryman, to paint and illustrate what his Community of Tomorrow would look like. The artist's touch brings beauty to order. Walt built his career around animation and finding the best artists to enrich his films. So when it came to EPCOT, he made sure to do the same. Urban design was key in the development and marketing of EPCOT, as it was for Opa-locka. There is an obvious connection between Walt's vision of tomorrow—and making sure it would be presented in an aesthetically pleasing way—and Curtiss's vision for the pinnacle American Garden City and his desire for it to be whimsically themed. This artistic touch marks the capstone of the entire development of these two cities.

eXperimental Tip: Sometimes it seems the art of the future is just as important as the future itself. We want our future to be not only bright, but beautiful. This eXperimental Tip delves into this desire, as it mirrors an aspect that we have seen before. As Glenn Curtiss hired urban designer Bernhardt Emil Muller to help with Opa-locka, Walt Disney turned to friend and long-term Disney team member Herbert Dickens Ryman to help with the design work on EPCOT. While Walt and Curtiss wanted inspiration for urban design, urban design is more than just making something aesthetically pleasing; it is the conceptualization of city features, including public spaces, infrastructure, transportation, landscapes, and community facilities. Additionally, urban design is the artistic assemblage of an urban plan. To venture further into this question we can turn to James Rojas as he explores this idea in his blog post, "Why Urban Planners Should Work with Artists." Rojas noted, "The building blocks of a city comprised more than simply structures, streets, and sidewalks but equally encompassed personal experience, collective memory, and narratives." The involvement of urban design into urban planning transforms mere infrastructure into place, as Rojas puts it. This also brings me back to two other topics we touched on. The first is Arthur Radebaugh's comic strip and his presentation of the future in a way to attract close to 20 million readers. The ability to attract that amount of viewers may have been brewed by his experience in marketing, through illustrating material for Detroit automakers. The second past topic is the future as portrayed in the movie *Meet the Robinsons*. Director Steve Anderson went for a more coloristic fun future, "think about an iPod instead of a metallic future" in his designs. As such, design not only plays a role in the cities we create today, but the cities we create for tomorrow. What role can artists have in framing community structures and our future?

Glenn Curtiss and Walt Disney are two men beyond their times, linked in a strange desire to turn from what they were known for into a vastly different endeavor—urban planning. I have yet to see a source that looked at both of these men in connection with each other, though they share much the same trajectory. Both died before their urban planning dreams could be reached. Although Curtiss's vision had been partially put to brick, Walt's did not get that far. Their ultimate goals were never truly realized.

In fact, Curtiss is more known for Miami Springs, as he did not fully realize his design goals as we saw with Opa-locka. The sad truth is once the U.S. government assumed control of Opa-locka, the city was left for naught. Opa-locka never fully recovered its shinning potential. It is an amazing look at an American City, and deserves a history on it and hopefully a bright future.

In contrast, Walt's plans manifested to something beyond his visions. Is Walt Disney World Resort what Walt wanted? No, but I do not think he would argue with the joy it brings children and adults. There have been trials and tribulations as to the value Walt Disney World brings beyond escapism. But still, the vestiges of Walt's vision remain, as can be seen by the commitment of its Cast Members. Looking back at Walt and Curtiss's visions is a testament to how dreams survive or die after their masters are gone.

eXperimental Tip: What drives these innovators to city planning? Is it solely financial gain or is there something more? Is it a sense of power and control over their own piece of earth? Are they playing the video game Sim City, which requires the player to engage in urban planning to secure the survival of their city throughout centuries, but in real life? Or is it something deeper? Author J.R.R. Tolkien once said, "We have come from God, and inevitably the myths woven by us, though they contain error, will also reflect a splintered fragment of the true light, the eternal truth that is with God. Indeed only by myth-making, only by becoming 'sub-creator' and inventing stories, can Man aspire to the state of perfection that he knew before the Fall. Our myths may be misguided, but they steer however shakily towards the true harbour, while materialistic 'progress' leads only to a yawning abyss and the Iron Crown of the power of evil." Is this what led men like Curtiss and Walt to urban design, a move away from materialistic progress and towards the sub-creator in hopes of redemption and to a closer understanding of our own origins? Bold questions, I know.

CHAPTER 12
In the Wake of Walt: Disney's Retroventurism

We are in the home stretch now. The remaining chapters in this book explore the ideas of retroventurism and serve as my final call to action. We leave behind the direct insertions of business law topics and move into a place where we infuse what we have learned and watch it achieve motion. This chapter itself is a focus on practical retroventurism, which is the inspired fulfillment of an original plan but not to exact specifications as laid out. And not just any retroventurism, but the Disney company's. We start to see how Walt's plan for EPCOT unfolds as dictated by those who came after him and look for pieces of his vision in the world that was created in his wake. Some items can be directly traced to the EPCOT Film and Walt's plan while others are more in recognition to the idea of "always be in a state of becoming." We look at both in earnest. Before we do, let us discuss the elements the Disney company directly followed from Walt's plan in the creation of the Walt Disney World Resort.

While Walt's exact vision for EPCOT did not end up in Walt Disney World's plans, the Disney company did directly implement some of Walt's foundational ideas for the Florida Project as described in the EPCOT Film and internal notations. These direct ideas included the creation of Reedy Creek Improvement District with its associated cities and the building of Magic Kingdom. The creation of these serve as a representation of a direct fulfillment of Walt's plan. Their creation and construction would have been completed in a similar manner if Walt had lived. As such, these elements, the Improvement District, the cities of Bay Lake and Reedy Creek (Lake Buena Vista), and Magic Kingdom, rest outside of retroventurism, for they were actually implemented almost in congruence with the original planner's ideal. Of course there are deviations; the Improvement District and its twin cities did not allow for the School of Tomorrow, but Roy had gained everything else Walt could have realistically wanted from the Florida legislature. Another slightly modified element is the Magic Kingdom that was built in Disney is not as an ancillary piece as Walt had envisioned but serves as the main draw, which, much to Walt's chagrin, probably would have been the case anyway, as it is what the people really wanted to see built. Any way one slices it though, these elements are a direct adherence and true to form to Walt's general plans as laid bare before his death.

In a similar vein, there is an additional element the Disney company fully implemented but was also one they expanded upon. That is the conversation of the wetlands in the Improvement District and the creation of sanctuaries for additional flora and fauna as well. The maintaining and preserving of conservation areas was part and parcel of Disney's package for the Improvement District legislation. It is also currently a major function of the Improvement District's administration. According to Disney's official publications, approximately one-third of its property has been set aside for conservation to provide "a home for animals like gopher tortoises, nearly 70 butterfly species, and purple martins—small songbirds that travel to Walt Disney World Resort to raise their young before flying more than 6,000 miles to the Brazilian rainforest and back."

Additionally, Walt Disney World has two theme park attractions that act as sanctuaries. Their aquarium located at The Seas with Nemo & Friends in Epcot and the zoological park located at Disney's Animal Kingdom[59] theme park. Disney notes three hundred sea turtles have been nursed back to health at its facilities and returned to open waters. Additionally, the Animal Kingdom zoological park is home to a myriad of African species. They include lions, elephants, and giraffes, to name a few. Disney engages in both research and conservation at Animal Kingdom, developing technology to aid in anti-poaching as well as attempts to reintroduce animals into the wild in areas where they had previously gone extinct. As such, the sanctuary portion most likely exceeded the expectations of Walt's original vision and is worthy of inclusion in this chapter.

There are several pieces of Walt's plan that were developed in the spirit of his original plans, as opposed to direct adherence of it. These other developments are Disney's exercise in practical retroventurism, gaining inspiration from Walt's plan but not being controlled by it. One item that falls into practical retroventurism that we have covered in detail is EPCOT Center, now Epcot. Thus, we will bypass EPCOT Center in this chapter to avoid repetition.[60] EPCOT Center is the most pivotal form of Disney's take on retroventurism, but it is also merely the cusp. There are a slew of projects and attractions that were either inspired by Walt's EPCOT or derived from it. Some of the projects merely got to the planning stages, others were built but disappeared with the passing of time, and others were built and remain a vital

59 Animal Kingdom and Disney's Hollywood Studios are the other half of the four theme parks at Walt Disney World, Epcot and Magic Kingdom being the two most discussed in this book.
60 There is an argument that the spirit of EPCOT Center is actually a standalone object. In the words of Joshua Harris, curator/creator of E82 Legacy, "A commonly-held misconception is that EPCOT Center was conceived only after the impracticalities of a vast corporately-controlled city were discovered and therefore the Center was created, not as the culmination of Walt's dream but as compensation for it. In fact, the origins of EPCOT Center not only run concurrently to the community of tomorrow but vastly precedes it." E82 will be explored later as well.

part of Walt Disney World to this day.[61] Which brings us to our first Disney created practical retroventurism construct, the Contemporary Resort.

The Contemporary Resort is the heart of Walt's EPCOT in a microcosm, and that is why I bring it up first. The Contemporary is the only resort where Disney's monorail system actually has a stop inside the hotel. Much like in Walt's envisioned Emerald Green Transportation Station, the Contemporary's transportation hub is located directly inside the middle of its central structure. On the level of the Contemporary's monorail stop is a restaurant and shopping options. There are currently three shopping locations on this level, one an upscale store, the other a child friendly shop, and the third a convenience store utilized by guests of the hotel. The check in for hotel guests is not actually on this level, but is located on the ground floor where vehicle transportation arrives. The Contemporary has several nightlife options for both the hotel guests and Disney World visitors alike.[62]

Even the building of the Contemporary is reminiscent of Walt's ideal for utilizing different forms of technology. The Contemporary utilized an interesting construction method, that of modular rooms. Modular rooms usage means the rooms were pre-constructed and then fitted into place by the use of cranes after the main structure of the Contemporary had been completed. There was once a rumor that modular rooms used by the architects could be removed in whole and in their place a brand-new room slid in. It appears though that this was mere rumor and conjecture based upon its modular design.

The Contemporary Resort, with its centralized transportation hub that delivers guests and visitors to shops and a restaurant, really does ring true to Walt's vision of his central resort in the Experimental Prototype Community of Tomorrow. Undoubtedly, it is a much more minimal display than what Walt had envisioned, but homage it is. It serves to remind us with a whisper and wink what Walt truly was after.

One item that saw a lot of effort on the part of the Disney team to keep alive from Walt's original plans was the transportation elements. We have already seen the first one, the monorail, as it glided seamlessly into the Contemporary Resort. The monorail system at Walt Disney World is something Walt would most likely be impressed by as it transverses across the

---

61 The Original E.P.C.O.T website (www.the-original-epcot.com) maintains a wealth of information on Walt Disney's original vision for EPCOT and the parts that were implemented. Available there are videos, photographs, and renderings. I advise visiting this website and taking a tour of all its offerings.

62 In this sense, with the Contemporary Resort and its amenities and transportation hub, we almost catch a hint of the theoretical retroventurism tour of Walt's EPCOT I imagined earlier. I myself have been a passing visitor of the Contemporary, arriving on the monorail, disembarking, visiting stores, and enjoying night life before venturing on my way.

property, delivering people to transportation stations near theme parks, next door to resorts, and, as noted, even inside a resort. It in fact exceeds in some sense what Walt had planned for EPCOT.

In the EPCOT Film, the monorail was to act as the spine of the transportation system, running from the entrance complex through the industrial complex, then into EPCOT, and ending at Magic Kingdom. The monorail itself had already featured at Disneyland California for some time, but not on the scale it would be built in Florida. The Walt Disney World Resort monorail has a track of almost fifteen miles, with around 50 million Disney guests traveling on the monorail each year. The Original E.P.C.O.T website lays out the various current tracks: (1) *Express*; (2) *Resort*; and (3) *Epcot*. The Express service runs between the Magic Kingdom and the Walt Disney World's current Entry Complex. The Resort track makes stops at the Magic Kingdom, the Entry Complex, Disney's Polynesian Resort, Disney's Grand Floridian Resort and Spa, and Disney's Contemporary Resort.[63] The last route is the Epcot route, which runs between Epcot and the Entry Complex. The Disney team did not stop its transportation push with the monorail, as it sought to include other items dreamt by Walt.

In the Magic Kingdom theme park, there is a small transportation implementation that pays homage to Walt's business plan, the WedWay PeopleMover. The PeopleMover was never made into a standalone transportation system on Disney property, unlike the monorail. In the Magic Kingdom it serves as an attraction ride above the Tomorrowland area. A fantastic feature of Walt Disney World Magic Kingdom PeopleMover ride is that guests get a glimpse of a portion of the Progress City model, which was moved from California to Florida. Although the model no longer moves and only a portion of the original survives, it is a neat treat for riders, and I would suggest visiting it. The transportation elements did not end with the PeopleMover or the monorail. For a time, Walt Disney Resort had a full functioning airport as Walt had envisioned, if not to the scope he had wanted.

Walt's original vision called for a large scale four-runway regional airport; what was constructed was a STOLport. The STOLport was not as grand as Walt envisioned but was still special in its own right. STOLs were not jets. The acronym refers to Short Take-Off and Landing aircraft. These aircraft could land on or take off from shorter airstrips than standard commercial jetliners at the time. STOLs were envisioned for short, rapid transportation, even seen as a means for reducing road traffic in areas. As such, the use of

---

63 A fun side note, there is an unofficial "adult" Disney activity called the monorail pub crawl, which includes venturing along the *Resort* monorail track and stopping at each of the four main resorts to buy and enjoy an available signature resort drink.

STOLport did fit in Walt's vision for reducing the reliance on the automobile, and at a minimum STOLport is a name that draws some attraction to it. Disney's STOLport maintained scheduled flights to the larger airports in Orlando and Tampa, the flights being provided by Shawnee Airlines.

The STOLport functioned for about a two-year period. One amazing feature was a surprise for guests arriving by air. When a STOL would land, grooves and small bumps built into the runway played the tune "When you wish upon a star." While small in stature, the STOLport was still a nod to Walt's originally planned airport. Again, like the Contemporary and the PeopleMover, it was not a fulfillment of Walt's vision but a representation of it applied to the current desire and needs of the Walt Disney World development team. The STOLport is no longer in use and parts of where it stood are being repurposed. With that said, you can recall Roy secured the right for a full airport from the Florida legislature, a right they still have, in case Disney wanted to ever try this again.

As far as elements in the theme parks themselves, one item that is both a direct implementation and an exercise in practical retroventurism is the AVAC systems and the Utilidors located under Magic Kingdom. The Utilidors are underground corridors that are on the first floor of the Magic Kingdom. In fact, Magic Kingdom is built on top of an entire ground level series of hallways. These hallways allow Cast Members to travel to and fro unseen by guests of the theme park. Right above the heads of Cast Members in the Utilidors runs a series of pipes that represent the AVAC (Automated Vacuum Collection system), which are waste disposal systems. Waste disposal was a specifically requested item in the Improvement District legislation, and the engineers of the Magic Kingdom utilized this right. As the Original E.P.C.O.T webpage describes, "[t]his system is still in use today with 17 collection points around Magic Kingdom and an underground system of vacuum tubes. Every 15 minutes, trash is sucked at a speedy 60 miles per hour to a compactor located behind Splash Mountain." From that final location, the trash is collected and removed away from Magic Kingdom. It is truly an engineering marvel, and something Walt had shown an interest in.

eXperimental Tip: If you have seen the EPCOT Film, and followed along in other aspects, are there any other items you think we can add to this list of practical retroventurism? Maybe there is some aspect of a particular park you know about that you can pinpoint a connection to Walt's plan. If you find one, do not be shy. Let me know! One item is the entire property itself is almost a fully functional city, which in essence is what Walt envisioned. The property consists of over thirty hotels and resorts, four state-of-the-art theme parks, 4 golf courses, sports complexes, two water parks, close to eight hundred camp sites, a lake with water transport, and self-enclosed transportation systems. The Resort's ability and propensity for self-reliance was put on display as it served as "bubble" for the NBA playoffs during the coronavirus pandemic in 2020. For additional understanding of scope, Reedy Creek Improvement District contains over 40 roadway bridges, five pedestrian bridges, three parking garages, 9,000 parking spaces and over 30 miles of roadways. With so many moving parts and so many visitors located on the property, there is a valid argument that the entire property is actually closer to Walt's EPCOT vision than many believe.

This just in, read all about it, the Disney Skyliner is operational! Although not included in any discussion of Walt's EPCOT Film, I personally feel the newly operational Disney Skyliner is a nod to Walt's "always be in a state of becoming," and to the catch all provision of the Reedy Creek Improvement District that allotted for new technologies. The Disney Skyliner is a state-of-the-art gondola system that currently connects Disney's Hollywood Studios and International Gateway at Epcot to the following Resorts: Disney's Caribbean Beach Resort, Disney's Art of Animation Resort, Disney's Pop Century Resort, and Disney's Riviera Resort. The Skyliner runs on almost two miles of track. Walt's desire to continue developing new modes of transportation to inspire guests of the park is emulated with the Disney Skyliner, and I truly believe that the Skyliner was born of the desire to reduce vehicle traffic in the park from resorts not connected via the monorail, as a nod to Walt's automobile traffic concerns.

Disney Springs is an additional element that appears to be generally derived from Walt's plans, if not with a specific nod. The area has had numerous names, including Downtown Disney and Disney Village Marketplace. It includes retail, dining, and entertainment areas as well and music and sport complexes. To the south of Disney Springs are several architecturally distinct office buildings, in addition to the Team Disney Administration Building and the Walt Disney World Casting Center. There is a walk-in medical care facility, as well as the residential portion of the City of Lake Buena Vista in proximity. The City of Lake Buena Vista includes the Administration Area, which is used for production, maintenance, engineering, and administrative activities. It consists of warehouses, office buildings, communications centers, substations, even an employee softball field as well as a childcare facility.

There is an interesting under layer to Disney Springs as well. The themed shopping center was originally planned to be a functioning community, modeled in part after EPCOT. It was to be called the Lake Buena Vista Village; plans and even a model were drawn up for the community. The archivists at the Original E.P.C.O.T have collected photographs and information concerning Lake Buena Vista Village. As late as the mid-1970s, Disney's business plan for the Lake Buena Vista Village property included the following goals: (1) To build an activity-oriented "transient" home community; (2) To develop commercial, industrial and institutional areas that will serve both local and regional demands; (3) To develop unifying transportation elements that tie the community together; (4) To build with distinctive, innovative designs to the extent possible within the limitations imposed by land development economics, financing, and marketing; (5) To maintain a high degree of flexibility to respond to unforeseen opportunities inherent in these unique conditions; (6) To build a community with woods, waterways, trails, fields and active recreation; and (7) To build commercial, industrial, and institutional areas. The plans were bold, but also limited in scope as compared to Walt's EPCOT directly. But we still see EPCOT's stamp with mentions of "distinctive, innovative designs," "unifying transportation systems," and "commercial, industrial, and institutional areas." These terms bear the hallmarks of Walt's EPCOT.

Lake Buena Vista Village was to have four focused communities, each with its own architecture, accommodations, and a recreational center. The focuses were based on recreational activities: (1) tennis; (2) boating; (3) horseback riding; (4) golf. The designers even created a Multi-Modal Station, a transportation hub, where the monorail and PeopleMovers stations would converge. This is in a similar vein to EPCOT's central transportation hub in the Emerald Resort. As to functionality, residents would still be temporary in the Village as well. Author Sam Gennawey notes that Lake Buena Vista Village was not as ambitious as EPCOT.

An interesting and overlooked element with Lake Buena Vista Village was the timing. Plans for the Village can be seen as early as 1967, the year after Walt's death. As such, the Village was either in replacement of Walt's EPCOT or was to be built in concurrence or prior to EPCOT. The Village could have represented the satellite residential community noted in Walt's plan. I cannot say for certain though. While Lake Buena Vista Village did not get built, it is the prototype to the two later communities Disney would build, which are Celebration and Golden Oak, as discussed in previous chapters.

I say this because even as much as correlations were made between Celebration and Walt's EPCOT by the Disney company itself, and even my own comparison of both Celebration and Golden Oak to Walt's vision, they are not truly acts of practical retroventurism when applied to Walt's initial ambition. However, if we compare Celebration and Golden Oak to Lake Buena Vista Village, that is a completely different conversation. We can definitely draw parallels between the two communities, with their host of amenities and residential-focused mindset. As a result, Celebration and Golden Oak are evidence of a practical retroventurism of Lake Buena Vista Village, and as much as the Village was meant to be a dash of Walt's EPCOT, vestiges of Walt's vision seeped into the two communities actually built.

> eXperimental Tip: My use of Lake Buena Vista Village does not end there. The Village has much more in common with a community we have discussed previously, which is Opa-locka. It would be a fun exercise to compare the two—in fact the comparisons are quite equal. You can definitely engage in more research on both communities to unpack this. One item of difference is that Glenn Curtiss did begin construction, while Lake Buena Vista Village was converted to a shopping center focus. A side point on this is that this was another This is It! moment. Learning of Lake Buena Vista Village was a revelation to me and my plan of building a final project for my business law class around EPCOT. It honed my idea not to simply have students tell me how EPCOT could work, but move the question to them if you had the chance to pitch your own special district plan, what would you build? What laws would you need control over or have waived? The Lake Buena Vista Village opened my eyes to the alternative plans available and the many directions one can go. I no longer had to live in Walt's vision but could use his help to encourage others to achieve so much more.

The Disney MagicBand is the last element I want to touch on that is derived from Walt's visions, albeit indirectly. According to author and historian Steve Mannheim's research, Walt also envisioned EPCOT to be a cashless society. Walt was referencing computer systems, and during

Mannheim's 2002 book *Walt Disney and the Quest for Community*, this would seem to connect to credit card systems. Since that time though, Walt Disney World has actually taken this one step further with the advent of MagicBands. MagicBands are bracelets that contain a microchip and allow Disney to link many different activities, creating a seamless experience for its guests. Guests at resorts can attach their credit card to the MagicBand, and when traveling throughout the property use the MagicBand to purchase items without the need for removing their cash or credit card from their wallet. Additionally, the MagicBand also works in other aspects of the guest experience, such as a room key, a mode to sync photographs taken by Cast Members (PhotoPass), park entrance tickets (and the FastPass option), as well as used to automatically open gate entrance mechanisms to the resorts, and it coordinates with the guests' resort account if they have one.

It is also not simply ease of purpose and altruism for Disney with the MagicBands, but allows for an ease of spending. Much like credit cards, a MagicBand allows for a dilapidation of funds without the physical and tactile sense of watching cash deplete from your wallet. Another interesting aspect of the MagicBand is that the charges are not immediately reflected in the person's bank account, though they can be tracked through Disney applications. What occurs is that once a guest makes their final departure from Disney property, the total cash expenditures are calculated and then charged to the guest's bank account so the guest does not feel the brunt of their expenditures while at the park, presumably leading to increased expenditures. But, as discussed previously, Disney is a for-profit enterprise, and EPCOT as envisioned by Walt would have been the same. As such, we cannot dismiss MagicBands from being a derived element of Walt's vision solely because it is also a great tool for increasing customer expenditures.

> **eXperimental Tip:** From hyper-capitalization to communism, images of the financial future are as wide and varied as one can imagine, even back in Walt's time. As writer A.M. Gittlitz notes, "Science fiction and futurism entered their 'golden age' by the 1950s and '60s, both predicting the bright future that would replace the Cold War. Technological advances would automate society; the necessity of work would fade away. Industrial wealth would be distributed as a universal basic income, and an age of leisure and vitality would follow. Humans would continue to voyage into space, creating off-Earth colonies and perhaps making new, extraterrestrial

friends in the process." The other side of Disney's worrisome hyper-capitalization model spinning out of control is Gene Roddenberry and the eventual economics of his creation, *Star Trek*. The *Star Trek* future created by Roddenberry is devoid of scarcity, thus allowing for exploration of self and outer space. As Noah Smith puts it, "The rise of new technology means that all the economic questions will change. Instead of a world defined by scarcity, we will live in a world defined by self-expression. We will be able to decide the kind of people that we want to be, and the kind of lives we want to live, instead of having the world decide for us. The *Star Trek* utopia will free us from the fetters of the dismal science." As writer Tim Worstall notes, Smith's ideas are on par with Karl Marx, best known for his Communist Manifesto. As such, based upon reasonings similar to Smith's and those addressed by author Manu Saadia and his book *Trekonomics*, we are turned into the idea that *Star Trek's* economic principles are at its most basic sense pure and true communism. If you recall from an earlier eXperimental Tip on fascism, I quoted Futurist Rose Eveleth, stating, "[t]here are lessons to be learned for today's technologists and futurists in Marinetti's manifesto, and it would be foolish to ignore them." Can this also be true of fans of *Star Trek* and the move toward progressive socialism, and what others fear as eventual communism, in some sectors of America? Did futuristic outlooks like *Star Trek* make this more palatable to some? I don't know. There are deeper questions at work here, but in the words of the fantastic Mr. Spock, "Fascinating, Captain."

MagicBands offer a technological experience many guests are not accustomed to, comporting with the prototype ideals of EPCOT. Guests will return home talking about how they used their bracelet for everything during their stay at Walt Disney World. Walt instilled an ethos of "always be in a state of becoming," and the MagicBands truly are a reflection of that.[64]

This chapter took us on a journey of what was built following Walt's plan

---

64 Interestingly enough, smart phones are moving a quicker pace that MagicBands. As such, Disney has begun to move a vast amount of the technical elements of the MagicBands (as new as they may be) onto its Disney app.

for his visionary city, the Experimental Prototype Community of Tomorrow. As we can see, some of Walt's visions were incorporated fully, while others served as inspiration. Practical retroventurism allows us to examine how dreams are interpreted to fit the reality that comes after (i.e. practicalness). The Disney company did indeed take some of Walt's general ideas and apply them going forward. Now we will get to see others take up the mantle outside of the Disney company, and this will illuminate the importance of Walt's original vision.

CHAPTER 13
The Future World of Now

This chapter takes us to a new frontier, the Future World of Now. In the pages that follow, we visit various futures. Some we can see the foundations being laid while others are still in the conceptual stage. In doing so, we remove ourselves from the shadow of Disney's theme parks and property and enter a world outside of Disney's control. We have learned that Walt and his EPCOT laid the work for much and more, and we are able to examine his business plan, build upon it, and also see it built upon by the Disney company. However, others outside of the Disney theme park umbrella have taken up retroventurism when it comes to Walt's EPCOT. These others began to think of ways to expand on the ideals forged in the crucible of Walt's imagination and take them in new directions. As we will now see, this book is merely one form of practical retroventurism. There are many others. It is my hope you will add your own. Join me as we retroventure with the Visionaries of Now. What has Walt's dream inspired in others to make real, make believe, or even make hopeful?

The big screen, movies—well, two movies in particular—took on the task of Walt's vision for EPCOT. The first movie I touched on in a previous eXperimental Tip, and that is the 2015 Disney movie *Tomorrowland*. That film's story was penned by the trio of Brad Bird,[65] Damon Lindelof,[66] and Jeff Jensen. *Tomorrowland's* storyline as described by Disney Studios is as follows: "Bound by a shared destiny, a bright, optimistic teen bursting with scientific curiosity and a former boy-genius inventor jaded by disillusionment embark on a danger-filled mission to unearth the secrets of an enigmatic place somewhere in time and space that exists in their collective memory as *Tomorrowland*." Tomorrowland is the name of a themed location inside Magic Kingdom, and it is undoubtedly from that themed location where Brad Bird and team got the name of their film. However, I feel the movie's roots lie elsewhere in the Disney ethos, and that is EPCOT. A review of the film and its background will give you glimpses beyond its themed location name and steer you toward Walt's version of the Experimental Prototype Community of Tomorrow.

65 Brad Bird is a prime Disney story and screenplay writer; his projects include numerous Disney and Pixar tentpoles such as the *Incredibles* and *Ratatouille*. As well as a serving on Pixar's Senior Creative Team.
66 Damon Lindelof is known for his creative roll on the TV show *Lost*, and the 2019 adaptation of the *Watchmen*, where Jeff Jensen also joins him.

Brad Bird gave an interview as to his inspiration for *Tomorrowland*, in which he indicates that he was enticed by Walt's vision of EPCOT. Specifically, Bird found an interest in Walt trying to achieve EPCOT towards the end of his life. As Bird expounds, "The fact that he did these things in his last moments meant something to me." Bird naturally wondered, what if Walt had lived? "You know, what if the alternate universe of him living another twenty years and getting to realize these things? You know. It touched me and I wanted to see if we could kind of represent the essence of it without being that specific." As such, it was no surprise that one receives inklings of Walt's EPCOT vision throughout the film, including the early portions of the film where the City of Tomorrow is represented.

Joshua L. Harris, the creator and contributor to the E82 Legacy website, has an intriguing outlook on *Tomorrowland*. He notes that film itself is a conduit to Tomorrowland, not merely a fanciful depiction of it. He decries, "[W]hether you loved or hated the film, nearly every critic and layperson has complained that you don't get to spend enough time in the title location. Which I would contend is the entire point!" Harris turns to Thomas Edison, who is referenced in the movie, and "famously said, 'Discontent is the first necessity of progress.'" Harris concludes, "[e]ither by design, or divine intervention, one should leave this movie feeling hungry and not satisfied." Harris views the movie as encouraging the viewer to take the leap to "create their own Tomorrowland." This mentality is a strong element of retroventurism, to take on the role of the creator, and I appreciate its mention with a review of *Tomorrowland*.

This connection between *Tomorrowland* and Walt's EPCOT is also reinforced by others who have reviewed the movie. The film reviewers at The Disney Movie Review, an independent fan site, take the following approach: "*Tomorrowland* is the savior of Walt's dream for EPCOT." The reviewers note that instead of creating a physical EPCOT, the movie *Tomorrowland*, "suggests the future is all around you if you have the right tools to see it." They continue to conclude, "EPCOT, like Disneyland, was never supposed to be completed, *Tomorrowland* gives each of us a role in creating the future we want to live in." Again, we are given a nod to assume the role of creator, which I am enthralled about and find extremely important. Now, the one issue I do take up with The Disney Movie Review is where they note, "All of these ideas have been presented before in Disney films, but none of them have been tied so directly to Walt, the theme parks and the dream of EPCOT." In fact, I do believe there was another film...

The second movie actually came out before *Tomorrowland*, and it is the 2007 animated feature *Meet the Robinsons*. The movie is based upon a book by William Joyce, *A Day with Wilbur Robinson*. To quote Bill Desowitz from his interview with the creative minds behind the film, it is "about an orphan named Lewis who's a genius inventor on a quest to find his birth mother, who's whisked away in a time machine by a mysterious kid named Wilbur Robinson who needs him to save the future from a strange Bowler Hat Guy." It is a wonderful film, generally, and has a unique aspect in that the time machine takes Lewis to a place called Todayland. (Todayland was another name I felt I could use for this chapter.) Director Steve Anderson specifically noted that, "[f]or Todayland, which is our homage to Walt Disney's Tomorrowland, think about an iPod instead of a metallic future." The iPod reference being to the colorful hues involved. Unlike Brad Bird, Steve Anderson makes no direct reference to Walt's EPCOT in any interview I could find, but with a detailed examination of the film itself, one can see representations of it.

This idea is dutifully tackled by Cesar Jimenez's blog Science-Faction. In a blog post titled, "Disney's *Meet the Robinsons*…a Much Better *Tomorrowland* Movie?" Jimenez takes on the hopeful aspirations of Walt's futuristic compass and compares the two films as to which captured it best. While Jimenez's focus is on the themed area Tomorrowland, he does mention EPCOT. I believe the comparisons of the two films is best connected to Walt's vision of the Community of Tomorrow. Jimenez looks upon Walt's outlook for tomorrow, and in him doing so, this undoubtedly leads me to a discussion on Walt's enunciated vision of the future, which I believe finds representation in EPCOT.

Jimenez, as to the comparison between *Tomorrowland* and *Meet the Robinsons*, contends, "*Meet the Robinsons* is actually MUCH closer to what a *Tomorrowland* film SHOULD HAVE been." As Jimenez rightly states, "MOST of [*Meet the Robinsons*] takes place in the future, where we get to see a bunch of advanced technology, art deco designs, shiny elements, flying cars, and everything is all bright, beautiful, cute, colorful, and fun." Jimenez points out the existence in the future of Disney transportation elements such as monorails and the PeopleMover. Additionally, one of the recurring themes throughout the film is a Walt Disney quote of "keep moving forward."[67]

While Jimenez tries to steer the conversation to focus on Tomorrowland,

---

67 This is a part of a much larger quote attributed to Walt Disney, "There's really no secret about our approach. We keep moving forward—opening up new doors and doing new things—because we're curious. And curiosity keeps leading us down new paths. We're always exploring and exper-imenting. At WED, we call it Imagineering—the blending of creative imagination with technical know-how." Wonderful quote, and I say attributed because I cannot independently confirm where Walt originally said this. Although the Disney company itself promotes this quote as directly com-ing from him. There are some notations that this quote is actually created by WED Industries itself and not Walt.

the themed area in Magic Kingdom, I think he would have been best served to draw the discussion towards EPCOT. As Jimenez finds, "Tomorrowland, the land [i.e. the themed area] itself, was about the possibilities of the future, how technology has evolved over time and what this could mean for future innovations." In fact, that quote more resembles Walt's vision for EPCOT as "always be in a state of becoming." But it is the focus on how people live in this film where I really see the connection. As Jimenez continues, *Meet the Robinsons* is about "a future where technology has become more advanced and has made people's lives better and easier." The focus on how people live is what draws *Meet the Robinsons'* ideals closer to Walt's EPCOT. Jimenez joyfully concludes *Meet the Robinsons* is about "technology and innovations, leading to great new heights." In fact, those words could have been an EPCOT advertisement as much as a Tomorrowland endorsement.

> eXperimental Tip: I drive two flying cars, how is this possible? We have before us two different versions of the same future vision. Comparing and contrasting *Tomorrowland* and *Meet the Robinsons* and their depictions of Tomorrowland/Community of Tomorrow is a fun exercise. The styles are very different, but you may find similarities under the hood of both films. As can be seen from Cesar Jimenez's blog, both take you to a future or otherworld destination. But what one finds there is the big question, as well as the underlying themes of the films. Check out Jimenez's blog if you can and see if you agree with him after watching the films. For additional research material, you can check out two books as well. One we have mentioned, which is William Joyce's illustrated work *A Day with Wilbur Robinson*, the other is a prequel penned by the *Tomorrowland* team of Brad Bird, Damon Lindelof, Jeff Jensen, and joined by Johnathan Case. I will leave you with a quote from *Meet the Robinsons*, which I feel sums up part of what I sought to create with the ethos of retroventurism: "Just because the past is painful doesn't mean the future will be."

It is also not just fiction where EPCOT retroventurism is utilized. People turned to the legal framework of Reedy Creek Improvement District to solve real world problems. Attorney and author Arin Greenwood composed a report on behalf of the Competitive Enterprise Institute discussing the

Disney's Improvement District. The goal of the report was to analyze whether the Improvement District model could be used to help save Florida's property insurance system. Florida's property insurance system has long been under stress due to the frequency of hurricanes and tropical storms that enter the area and the need to offer affordable insurance premiums to those who live in the state. For the report, Greenwood looks to a period in 2004 when Central Florida was hit by three successive hurricanes. These hurricanes ranged from categories 2 to 4, meaning the storms had a range of sustained winds from approximately 100 mph to 150 mph. Surprisingly, Disney suffered only $50,000 of damages during those storms, while the rest of the Central Florida, in Greenwood's words, was an unmitigated disaster. Specifically, billions of dollars of damages occurred throughout Florida, including loss of life. Yet, as noted, the Disney property remained practically unscathed and was able to continue operations in a short fashion.

Greenwood interviewed Ray Maxwell, the District Administrator for the Reedy Creek Improvement District, to ask why Maxwell thought the property was able to escape major damage. Together, Greenwood and Maxwell mapped out three answers, all dealing with the role the Improvement District plays on property and its relationship with Disney. First, there are strict and uniform building codes originating from the Improvement District and applied consistently throughout the Disney property. These codes are strictly enforced by Maxwell and his staff. Additionally, the Improvement District building code and safety teams worked with Disney from the very start of the building plans instead of simply coming later to note problem areas. The second answer to Disney's success is the vast amounts of wetlands on Improvement District property that help alleviate flooding. Flooding is a strong secondary storm variable that causes damage during a passing hurricane. The wetlands help soak up the additional flood waters. The helpful wetlands are regularly maintained by the Improvement District to ensure they can act effectively when needed. Greenwood uses a very Disney word to discuss the Improvement District's approach to flooding as "holistic."[68] The holistic ethos may connect to the eco-friendly notion of using the natural environment to help protect against natural disasters. The third and final item is the close relationship between the Improvement District as a quasi-government and its main resident, the

---

68 Holistic is a term you will see pop up in Disney company papers, but even more so by people describing what Disney does. "The Walt Disney Company is providing a holistic, memorable, and attractive brand experience through motion pictures, animations, theatrical and musical performances, vast media networks, interactive websites and games, toys and other merchandise, and the huge set up of recreational parks and resorts all over the world." —"How Disney Built An Empire By Designing Brand Experience" By Janil Jean , Dec 11, 2015.

Disney company. This allows the Improvement District to focus resources on hurricane preparedness (a main concern of Disney to ensure maximum operational capacity), while not having to answer to other taxpayers' or voters' concerns. Disney's main concern is the safety of its guests and to ensure it stays open, hence those are the Improvement District's main concerns as well.

In her report, Greenwood then takes the practical retroventurism leap, which is exciting to see. She asks such questions as, can the Improvement District model be used to save Florida insurance conundrum? and, would allowing more improvement districts like the Reedy Creek Improvement District to be built save Florida taxpayers money in the long run and help keep Florida's property insurance platform stabilized? Greenwood finds that if you tweak the Reedy Creek model by reducing some powers it has and then on the other hand limit residents' variables through contractual means (age and land use restrictions), it could work. The restrictions on residents would help narrow the focus of these newly-formed mini improvement districts. More importantly, if these mini improvement districts failed to work, the State legislature could step in and call the whole thing off. Greenwood finds the legislature would be better positioned to cancel out these mini improvement districts with less issues than the legislature would run into trying to cancel everything that was given to the Disney company in the 1960s. For me this was a fascinating use of an EPCOT generated idea being used to solve a real-world problem.

> **eXperimental Tip:** We know now that visions of the future can create answers for today. I cannot understate enough the importance in discovering Arin Greenwood's report for the creation of a final project for my business law students. It showed me elements of Walt's vision for EPCOT could be crafted to solve important tangible issues facing us today. To use Walt's words, none of that "blue sky" stuff, but issues that are at least easier to quantify. Greenwood's report is worth a read through in its entirety. The report gave me insights about the steps students would need to take to apply the EPCOT model, especially Disney's unique Improvement District, to a novel issue of their choice. It helped explore the hurdles and experiments that would need to be overcome and conducted in order to achieve desired results. In general, the report is a prototype of what I wanted my students to achieve with their own ideas. I owe a debt to that report.

Read through it. Do you think it would work?

There is one last retroventurism type I want to look at, and I pull two examples to do so. These final ones are not Walt's EPCOT retorventurists, but are in effect RetroCenturions (a play on my Retroventurism and the theme park EPCOT Center). Joshua L. Harris and Dr. Alan Bowers have developed two unique models in a quest to continue the importance of not only Walt's work, but that of Disney men like John Hench and Marty Sklar and their creation of EPCOT Center. RetroCenturions maintain a strong sense of importance to the original EPCOT Center theme park as it initially opened and existed prior to subsequent overhauls that moved it away from edutainment and solely into entertainment. The visions created by the RetroCenturions are extremely fascinating and show alternative uses of retroventurism.

Harris took his RetroCenturions role and applied it to a concept called E82: The EPCOT Legacy. It was developed over time through the use of his website bearing the same name. The 82 is a reference to the year EPCOT Center opened to the public. It is an expansive website that contains a multitude of experiences for its visitors. Tracking the origins of The EPOCT Legacy, Harris reiterates Walt's ability to create an idyllic theme park experience was translated towards the end of his life to plan to create a similar all-encompassing lifestyle. But with his death Harris notes, "Walt's concept would change hands (and heads) several times before reaching its final and most effective form. EPCOT Center opened in 1982." Harris laments that while EPCOT Center achieved much, "there are many more heights left to be scaled and unfortunately much of EPCOT Center's original vision has changed." EPCOT Legacy site tracks those changes from EPCOT Center becoming EPCOT and eventually Epcot.

While Harris is acutely aware that the nature of Epcot requires it be updated, as the future tends to arrive before we know it, Harris found, "the one thing that should never change is the ideals and principles on which the park was founded." It is to that loss of ideals and principles that E82 focuses on recapturing or, better yet, recentering. The website offers, "[a]n exploration of the many aspects and effects of Epcot's influence throughout its existence and it is also a forum for its future." It contains elements such as the E82 Institute. Whereby EPCOT Center was in many ways a blueprint for tomorrow, the E82 Institute will be a guidebook. A collection of ideas espoused by some of the greatest innovators are collected in the E82 Institute to help unpack the future we are heading towards.

One of the more intriguing elements is E82's art and music sections.

Collections of soundtracks to create "listening experiences" that focus on the Epcot Legacy is immensely innovative. Sound plays an important but not immediately noticeable part of our experience spectrum. The soundtracks are used to create moods. For example, one such mood is Christmas Time at Progress City. It is pure retroventurism to create a soundtrack for an unfinished visionary city at Christmas time. Bowers, our next RetroCenturion, agrees about the use of sound, noting songs provide a "narrative soundtrack" or "theme reinforcer." It truly is an interesting aspect of E82, coupled with the many other experiences offered there. E82, at the end of the day, is a unique application of retroventurism, and it strives toward a theme that is often repeated on the website and one that was drawn from an original ride at EPCOT Center, Horizons, "if we can dream it, we can do it!"[69]

As previously mentioned, the next RetroCeturion I wish to touch on is Dr. Alan Bowers.[70] His PhD dissertation offers a discussion into the utility of using Walt's vision and EPCOT Center as a means of creating a utopian-based curriculum for grade school children in addition to creating an updated model of EPCOT Center. As such, we have two competing excursions into retroventurism from one source, the curriculum creation, and EPCOT Reborn, as Bowers calls his second vision. Bowers's utopian focus is achieved by "tracing the evolution of EPCOT as an idea for a community that would 'always be in the state of becoming' to EPCOT Center as an inspirational theme park, this work contends that those ideas contain possibilities for how to interject utopian thought in schooling." In hopeful conveyance as to EPCOT Reborn, "it is [Bowers's] over-arching contention that the existing literature that focuses on Disney has missed something important: the potential of EPCOT to serve as a living model where teachers, students, decision-makers, etc. discuss 'possible futures' in a living laboratory."

Bowers sums up the relationship between Walt's EPCOT and EPCOT Center and their failed aspirations as such: "EPCOT Center asked the questions about tomorrow but then gave up and retreated to become another vehicle to mostly sell merchandise and promote current intellectual properties (IPs) such as Marvel and Pixar." As to Walt's EPCOT, "While the experimental city was never attempted, let alone realized, EPCOT Center at least displayed an effort into creating a hopeful curriculum."

---

69 Interestingly, this quote is often misattributed to Walt Disney, but it originated from Sheralyn Silverstein, who wrote it as part of a recruitment campaign her ad company was involved with doing for General Electric in 1981.

70 At the time of his dissertation, he is to be considered the not-quite-yet Doctor Bowers, but for ease of purpose I refer to Alan Bowers, Phd as Dr. Bowers regardless of the fact that I quote work done before his PhD.

In the vacuum left by Walt's EPCOT and EPCOT Center, Bowers creates a vision for EPCOT Reborn as a manifestation of his utopian curriculum, "A place where utopian curriculum goes beyond the school walls and into the present and the possible." While acknowledging the limitation of his ideas, Bowers does venture into a recalibration of ECPOT Center as a publicly-funded endeavor and turns to three areas of the original EPCOT Center of most interest to him, The Land, Journey into Imagination, and Horizons. I will travel with you to venture through EPCOT Reborn and explore its pavilions, but I do want to note an interesting aspect before moving forward, and that is the idea of the "Institute."

Harris's E82 has an element called an Institute, and EPCOT Reborn does as well. Bowers located an internal Disney company document from 1976 discussing a new vision for EPCOT. I will call this new vision E76. E76 had three parts: an Institute, a Theme Center, and Satellites. While I do not have access to the E76 reference document, the plans do ring true to layouts and press conferences held by then-Disney CEO Card Walker. It was during this time that we begin to see some of the first concrete representations that Disney would be moving away from Walt's EPCOT, which was a resident-focused city, and moving more towards a technological hub of today and tomorrow. Author Michael Crawford does an excellent job tracking Card Walker and the Disney company's moves and statements during this time. Crawford's research and narrative can be found on his website for Progress City, U.S.A.

E76 was to be structured to encourage and assist participation in EPCOT by industry, universities, public agencies, foundations, and other supporters of the general EPCOT philosophical concepts. Bowers found this model helpful for his EPCOT Reborn, "[t]his model helps foster utopian curriculum through the purposeful staging of interdisciplinary exhibits in invigorated pavilions which will host symposiums and conferences on building a sustainable future." Teachers, philosophers, scientists, and futurists coming together to rethink today and tomorrow.

As discussed earlier, one divergent aspect on EPOCT Reborn is that the management for this ideal would be publicly funded. I reached out to Bowers on this point, and he said that the choice was done to ease the whole approach. He mentions two items in his work for the choice of public funding: (1) a publicly funded EPCOT "divorces itself from the need to accept potentially troublesome dollars;" and (2) "to avoid the influence of profit seekers pushing their agendas." This is a unique take on other Disney focused retroventurism exercises, as most have drawn on private ownership as opposed to public.

eXperimental Tip: My father used to tell me an allegory: "In the Wild West the bandits would come around asking for money to not rob you of everything, and eventually a sheriff would come to town and ask for money from you to help protect you from the bandits." Privately funded vs. publicly owned, you lose both ways. This is an excellent topic to dig in to. As far as we have seen, most retroventurism plans have been circled around privately owned visions. This is obvious in theoretical retroventurism of Walt's EPCOT, which seeks to imagine the completion of a project per his general specifications and is also obvious in the Disney company's exercises in practical retroventurism. Where you can reach divergent sources of control is through practical retroventurism outside of the Disney company, where you forge a new path based upon old plans that may not be viable for you. Arin Greenwood makes an excellent notation about the troublesome nature of private funding and ownership over plans such as these, but she felt the ultimate ability of State government to sweep the rug out from under the operation held enough assurance over those troublesome issues. Alan Bowers goes headstrong into addressing government control because of the eventual issues that may pop up, including the idea of being turned into a solely money-making machine at the expense of the altruistic aims. Inherently, the Greenwood and Bowers projects are innately different, but they do raise a question as to which one would be ideal for a project like EPCOT. Machiavelli might say, "If you can never tell there is anything nefarious going on with the private enterprise, I am fine on private control." Do you argue for a more practical reality?

This chapter has shown us visions of the future, both in fiction and aims of practical relevance. One item that we saw referenced in this chapter was the idea of assuming the role as the creator. I was encouraged by seeing this language, as it fits so well into what my ethos of retroventurism entails. Retroventurism requires assuming the role of the creator and building upon a framework of the past. Another linked term in this chapter is the idea of

149

reaching new heights or the failure of past ventures that left heights unscaled. As such, these terms are a focus on the brighter tomorrow, but they also represent the climb. The climb is the hard part of retroventurism, for it is where pieces must be put together, mounted, changed, torn down, and built back up. It is also the most important part. The struggle is real, but it is vital.

In retroventurism, the journey may, in fact, be more important than the destination, regardless of how bright it is. "Ah, but a man's reach should exceed his grasp, or what's a heaven for?"[71] At the end of the day, it is that ideal of something beyond our ability, Nirvana, if you will, that is what excited me about EPCOT, retroventurism, and writing this book. We should always strive beyond our means. The understandable, but the unattainable. The best puzzles are the ones that you can never figure out. It is the desire to keep reaching for that which we may never grasp, not simply looking behind to recapture what we think we most desire, that makes us improve. It is our collective push as humankind for a brighter tomorrow that will make each new day better than the last. Learning from the past, not because we are doomed to repeat it, but because we can borrow the best parts to make a brighter tomorrow. That is retroventurism.

---

71 This line comes from *Andre del Sarto*, a poem by Robert Browning. I encourage you to investigate this poem. It contains one of my new favorite lines, "What does a mountain care."

Epilogue
Keep Moving Forward

In the documentary *Down to Earth with Zac Efron*, the actor and his health guru Darin Olien travel around the world, learning and experiencing healthy eating and living. A great show, but something besides the healthy message caught my eye. In the episode where the pair go to Puerto Rico, Zac is asked to sign his name on a wall. He does so after some moral reluctance, and then writes a message. That message was "keep moving forward." I mention that because I was watching the episode randomly while editing this book, and I saw him scribble those words. I felt fate stare at me. Researching it a bit more, I ran into a quote from Dr. Martin Luther King, Jr., who was known to end speeches with the refrain, "If you can't run, walk; if you can't walk, crawl, but keep moving forward!" You may also recognize those words from our discussion on *Meet the Robinsons*. Strong words, important words, great words to end with, but even better words to begin with.

We have made it! Well, you have made it. I've actually been sitting here the whole time waiting for you. Thank you for taking this journey, but we have come to what is actually only the beginning. It is from here that I launch a 1,000 EPCOTs. It is here that I take the ideas of the past and the understandings of business, mix them all together, and finally send you on your way.

This book contained basic elements of business law. In the chapters that came before we learned about the origins of business, the basics of contracts, and various types of business entities. We tackled topics not frequently addressed in business law texts, such as public relations law and business plans. We then took aim at core elements of all general business law courses ethics, regulations, and employment law. We even addressed immigration in relation to employment law.

With each topic you now have a basic understanding of their functioning in the greater business law system. Some topics we dived into great detail on very-small parts—remember the option contract and the Q-visa. The reality is there are thousands of threads into the quilt that make up business law. If there is something I mentioned in passing you want to learn more about, fantastic! Go forth, my page, and discover! Part of my job is done if that is the case, creating the desire in others to want to learn more is a testament to success for any Wizard Guide...Wait, what?

A Wizard Guide. You've never met one? Oh, I bet you have. Merlin, Yoda, Gandalf, Glinda the Good Witch, come on, Dumbledore, even Nicholas Cage...I am sure you can name others as well. Beginning each semester when I was teaching, I would tell my students my job is to lead them through the often obscure path of knowledge with a staff in one hand and light in the other. The light has a dual purpose, one for my benefit to find my way, and the other so you may easily follow. The staff, though, was for show because it made me sound like a Wizard Guide.

As your Wizard Guide for this book, I took you on a journey to discover retroventurism. Our main focus has been Walt Disney's original idea for EPCOT, but along the way we have met new and just as interesting faces and places. Glen Curtiss and his dream of Opa-locka, Radebaugh and Rodenberry, Rosamund and Vander, and we cannot forget our RetroCenturions either. This journey has been aided by modern cannon authors of the original EPCOT, Steve Mannheim, Sam Gennawey, Chad Emerson, and Richard Foglesong, each adding a different tone, taste, and experience to uncovering the depths of retroventurism. Whether it is imagining Walt's EPCOT completed by the use of theoretical retroventurism or by using past plans to create a business of tomorrow in practical retroventurism, we worked together with these creators, authors, innovators, and dreamers to get here.

It is interesting how after traveling with these individuals over the years, researching for my syllabus and eventually taking time to convert my syllabus into the work you see before you, I noticed similarities of individuals drawn to EPCOT. These individuals usually possess a strong pull towards either cooperative scientific futurism or urban land use, if not both.

Recall from my introduction, and various eXperimental Tips, this book was born from a final classroom assignment I would give my business law students. I want to go over that assignment in this Epilogue, so it can serve as a foundation for your own Experimental Prototype of...[Fill in the Blank].

My original assignment, which I would break up into parts to be worked on by my students, would be to develop a legislation package to be presented to a fictional local government to request the ability to establish a special district. This was done in a similar fashion to Reedy Creek Improvement District. This legislation package would then be prepared over the remainder of the semester as a long-term project. The final weeks would be devoted to turning in the legislation and also presenting the legislation to a panel of judges (other teachers or lawyers I know). It was a fun experience in my mind and given the length of time students could work on it, each project was well developed. The judges were always impressed.

I would draw up the game plan for what I wanted. We were not replicating the process exactly, and I made it more manageable to understand and work on. Some items I would condense, for example I would avoid the nuances of which rights could be allotted to the Improvement District and which could only be allotted to a city, instead they all could go into a general special district. I found a sample proposed legislation bill the students could use, but greatly reduced that down as well. We would still have the fun WHEREAS's all bills have, but I needed it to be functional for the students and not overly burdensome. As far as other items, I tried to keep what they were doing as close to what Walt, Roy, and the Disney team went through in planning and securing their legislation from Florida.

Our legislation would have the following parts: (1) *Sponsors Section*; the name of the student presenting the legislation would go here; (2) *Provision Title Section*, here they would all have the same generic title, which was the location followed by Special District, but then they would need an alternate title that reflected their proposed creation; (3) *Purpose Section*, this is the elevator pitch of the legislation, we would use some generalized language but they would need to sum up their creation in this section that could grab attention; (4) *Preamble Section*, oh, the WHEREAS's, this section had two purposes—one was to introduce why there is a need for the creation, for example, WHEREAS, the region's economy has been suffering due to the recent hurricane damage, and the other purpose was to show how the creation would help answer those needs in new and innovative ways; (5) *Enacting Clause Section*, this section was formalized throughout all projects, only difference is I would have the students pick the number of their legislation, Chapter 114, for example; (6) *Body of the Bill*, this section was more a standard student report than legislative-based, as here I would have the students describe their project to me; (7) *Legislative Purpose Section*, again this section would have some parts that would be the same for everyone, "the purpose of this statute is to create a special district that…" but I would then have the students put words in the mouth of the legislature, tell me what they would say if they approved your project, "The government recognizes the need for the special district because… and we will gladly support it because…"; (8) *Substantive Provisions of the Statute*, this section was devoted to all the rights they needed for their project to work, and describe why they needed those rights; (9) *Closing Section*, a formalized closing noting the date of their presentation as the date the law would be enacted.

To work through the project, I would break it down into three parts. The first part would include: (1) Basic idea for your improvement district; (2) Name of your improvement district; (3) start thinking about why it is important; and (4) begin inputing the information, especially all the similar generic language, into the legislation package. This may not seem like a lot but getting started is the hardest part. Thinking of that first idea. I was not asking them to build a better EPCOT. I wanted something completely new and different based upon the general framework Walt created. I wanted something that interested them that they felt was needed. What they created always surprised. I would see regional development centers, parks, a mixed-use college campus with space for elderly housing, immigration sanctuary city, a holistic hospital, shopping district with its own airport, even an organic cemetery as project ideas.

The second part of the project would build upon the first. After learning about what their basic idea was and why it was important, I could then help the students break down more nuanced issues to address. The second part of their project they would need to (1) develop an elevator pitch and (2) list all the rights they wanted. They would convert the elevator pitch into the Purpose Section. The rights part was fun. I would always mandate a set number a student had to include, for example eight rights/powers. They were encouraged to pick as many as they thought they would need to ensure stability and success in their project. In their legislation they would need to tell me why they would need a certain right. I would help flush this out for them if they needed the assistance.

Let me go over some examples of how the rights worked. If the student wanted to ensure stable water and sewer systems, the student would need to note a concern of theirs, for example "We want control over the water and sewer systems as a means to ensure any outside water main break would not prohibit operations in the special district and negatively impact our guests and thus the greater economic benefit to the area." For airport facilities, "To alleviate stress on regional and international airports near the special district based upon our visitor projections, we are requesting the right to construct airport and heliport facilities on the property." It was a neat way to have the students practice selling an idea without trying to outright offend someone of whom they were asking a favor.

The third part was finalizing everything and considering funding. They would be putting the ideas into a coherent structure that included the format I provided with the sample legislation bill. Funding was not included in the legislation, but when they presented their bill to the legislature (judges), they would need to think about how they were going to pay for it. For Walt's EPCOT it was three-fold; one was straight out of Disney's pockets, the other was seeking corporate partners, and the other was the issuance of bonds (and tax breaks), Disney would then breakeven and start using earnings from the Disney World to pay for itself. The idea was that Disney would not be asking the state for investment directly (yet indirectly with tax breaks). But I gave my students great leeway in their goals for obtaining money. Many went corporate sponsors or partners, some would be asking for the funding from the government, others would try to crowd source it, or seek donations as a not-for-profit, and many would combine elements. Some would go the Disney route of once it breaks even the project will be self-sufficient. It was a fun part of the exercise and made the project that more realistic when you start to talk money.

The students would then finish the semester by presenting their ideas to the legislature, whereby the guest judges would grade the presentations. The judges would also pick a project that was best presented. I would separately grade the legislative bills, in case one student had a great proposed bill but was not gifted at public speaking, so the grades would even out. It really was a rewarding experience in my mind, and I had a lot of fun working with my students through this.

If I had the time and resources I would have had my students do two things: one is to create a physical model of their proposed project and the second would be to pre-record a portion of their presentation focusing on what their special district is and use artistic renderings of it in the film. These requirements might prove burdensome in some aspects while beneficial in others. The pre-recording might help students who are not gifted at public speaking. As far as the design elements, while not all students are artists or designers, I think basic renditions could be done by all students. Whilst some students could exceed in those areas, no doubt, and surprise the judges with their designs. The model creation would probably be extremely time consuming as well, and again might prove burdensome, but would add a fantastic value for the judges to look at during the final presentation. Essentially, I would be asking the students to create their own Progress City model and EPCOT Film for their special district. They would then present the film, with the legislation, and the model for the judges. It would be amazing all around, though would most likely require a full semester to focus on.

That is what brought this book to its final version. I realized if I wanted to make this a full semester project, I would need to find ways to incorporate retroventurism throughout many themes of business law. I hit on many of the major sections of a standard course and even added some new ones. This allows the introduction of the final project from day one. This is what I now turn over to you.

If you are a professor looking to revitalize your business law class, this program is a perfect fit. Based upon the level, associate, bachelor, masters, or even beyond, it can be modified. The material in here can serve as a base board for more or less detailed instruction. It can even combine study fields, such as business students with, say, engineering students. The framework is there to create an unrivaled business law class, one that encourages students to think about how business and governments interact. What can business offer government, not as a competitor or subservient entity, but as a partner? You as the professor can go chapter by chapter, unraveling the mysteries of retroventurism for your students as they play the role of creator and develop their own special districts.

If you purchased this book for personal learning, I want you to give this a try as well. Retroventurism is for everyone, think of our RetroCenturions. What special district would you build? Is there a way you can use the ideals covered in this book to create a brighter tomorrow? I believe so, and I hope you will, too.

If it were up to me—and who knows, maybe after the publication of this book—I can create an International Retroventurism Design Fair where students from across the world compete with their own special district designs, developing their own project film and models to be exhibited for the retroventurism judges to decide who is best positioned to create that brighter tomorrow with their ideas. Heck, I could even try to get the final rounds of the competition to be in Epcot itself. Now that I believe is something Walt would've loved.

This brings my story to close, and yours to a beginning. My sincerest hope is that something in this ponderous tome inspired you to learn more. That the visionaries and visions we covered in these pages opened your eyes to the potential for a brighter future. You are now equipped with a basic understanding of business law, as well, and that will serve you well in your own personal future endeavors. It has been a pleasure writing this book and exploring these topics with you. If retroventurism has taught us one thing: it is the past is meant to not only be learned from, but also questioned and built upon.

Tomorrow awaits you, my friend. Best of luck! I know you will do great things!

BIBLIOGRAPHY

The sources contained herein are not an exhaustive list of every source I encountered during my quest to bring *Retroventurism* to life for you. This list, though, does provide a spring board to further your own research. This list contains many of the sources I mentioned throughout the chapters of this book.

Aimar, Stefania. *Coral Gables: A contemporary Urban Utopia.* PhD diss., IMT School for Advanced Studies, Lucca, 2016. http://e-theses.imtlucca. it/282/1/Aimar_phdthesis.pdf.

Allman, T.D. *Finding Florida: The True Story of the Sunshine State.* New York: Grove Press, 2013.

Baldwin, Simeon E. "American Business Corporations before 1789." *The American Historical Review* 8, no. 3 (1903): 449-465.

Beanland, Christopher. "Canned designs: Cars on roofs in Staines." *The Long + Short.* January 5, 2016. https://thelongandshort.org/cities/jelli-coe-glass-sky-motopia

Beard, Richard R. *Walt Disney's EPCOT Center: Creating the New World of Tomorrow.* New York: Harry N. Abrams, Inc., 1982.

Block, Alan A. *Masters of Paradise: Organised Crime and the Internal Revenue Service in the Bahamas.* New York: Routledge, 2019.

Bowers, Alan, *FUTURE WORLD(S): A Critique of Disney's EPCOT and Creating a Futuristic Curriculum.* PhD diss., Georgia Southern University, 2019. https://digitalcommons.georgiasouthern.edu/etd/1921.

Central Intelligence Agency. History of the CIA. Last modified March 23, 2013. https://www.cia.gov/kids-page/6-12th-grade/operation-history/his-tory-of-the-cia.html.

"Closer than We Think – 30 Minute Presentation." YouTube video, 31:21. Extract from a larger project. Posted by "Clindar," June 21, 2020. https://www.youtube.com/watch?v=lZH16NLcd3M.

Coady, C.A.J. "The Ethics of Armed Humanitarian Intervention." Peaceworks 45 (2002): 1-48.

Conservation Centers for Species Survival. "Disney's Animal Kingdom." Accessed September 10, 2020. http://conservationcenters.org/disneys-an-imal-kingdom/.

Corey, Amanda. "The J-1 Exchange Program: A Short Look at a Long History." October 17, 2017. https://iseusa.org/j-1-exchange-program-history/.

Crawford, Michael. "EPCOT: Origins – The Tripartite Plan, 1975." May 9, 2010. http://progresscityusa.com/2010/05/09/epcot-origins-the-tripar-tite-plan-1975/#identifier_6_3489.

Crouch, Tom D. "Glenn Hammond Curtiss." In Britannica. Last Modified July 19, 2020. https://www.britannica.com/biography/Glenn-Ham-mond-Curtiss.

Doyle, Alison. "Difference Between an Exempt and a Non-Exempt Employ-ee." Last Modified May 5, 2020. https://www.thebalancecareers.com/exempt-and-a-non-exempt-employee-2061988.

Dimmock, Mark and Andrew Fisher. *Ethics for A-Level.* Cambridge: Open Book Publishers, 2017.

Emerson, Chad Denver. *Project Future: The Inside Story Behind the Creation of Disney World.* United States of America: Ayefour Publishing, 2010.

Emerson, Chad D. "Merging Public and Private Governance: How Disney's Reedy Creek Improvement District "Re-Imagined" The Traditional Di-vision of Local Regulatory Powers", Florida State University Law Review 36, no. 2 (2009): 177-214.

Eveleth, Rose. "When Futurism Led to Fascism—and Why It Could Happen Again." *Wired.* April 18, 2019. https://www.wired.com/story/italy-futur-ist-movement-techno-utopians/.

Ferrise, Jennifer. "In the Olympic Village, Condoms Are Unlimited and the Swiss House Throws the Best Parties." *Instyle.* February 8, 2018. https://www.instyle.com/news/olympic-village-parties-condoms.

FitzGerald-Bush, Frank S. A Dream of Araby: Glenn H. Curtiss and the Founding of Opa-locka. Opa-locka: E. and J. Printing, Inc., 1976.

Fitzpatrick, David, "If You're Not Paying for it You're the Product." Novem-ber 23, 2010. https://lifehacker.com/if-youre-not-paying-for-it-youre-the-product-5697167.

Florida Department of Economic Opportunity. Introduction to Special Districts. Accessed September 9, 2020. https://floridajobs.org/com-munity-planning-and-development/special-districts/special-district-ac-countability-program/florida-special-district-handbook-online/introduc-tion-to-special-districts.

Florida Department of State Division of Corporations. Types of Business En-tities/Structures. Accessed September 9, 2020. https://dos.myflorida.com/sunbiz/start-business/corporate-structure/.

Florida State University College of Law. "Business Law Courses." Accessed September 10, 2020. https://law.fsu.edu/academics/academic-programs/juris-doctor-program/business-tax-law/business-law-courses.

Foglesong, Richard E. *Married to the Mouse: Walt Disney World and Orlan*do.

New Haven: Yale University, 2001.

"Futurism." In Tate, Accessed September 10, 2020. https://www.tate.org.uk/ art/art-terms/f/futurism.

Gennawey, Sam. *Walt Disney and the Promise of Progress City.* United States of America: Theme Park Press, 2014.

Gittlitz, A.M. "'Make It So': 'Star Trek' and Its Debt to Revolutionary Socialism." *The New York Times.* July 24, 2017. https://www.nytimes. com/2017/07/24/opinion/make-it-so-star-trek-and-its-debt-to-revolutionary-socialism.html.

Goldhaber, Mark. "History of the World, Part III." March 24, 2004. https:// www.mouseplanet.com/7112/History_of_the_World_Part_III.

Greenwood, Arin. "Florida's Reedy Creek Improvement District: Could private government help fix Florida's property insurance system?" Competitive Enterprise Institute. July 2010. https://cei.org/sites/default/files/ Arin%20Greenwood%20-%20Florida's%20Reedy%20Creek%20Improvement%20District.pdf.

Gross, Alexander. "Hermes—God of Translators and Interpreters." Accessed September 10, 2020. http://www.untoldsixties.net/hermes.htm.

Harris, Joshua L. "The EPCOT Legacy." Accessed September 10, 2020. https://www.epcotlegacy.com/.

Hitt, Tarpley. "In 2004, Disney sold the downtown of utopian Celebration, Florida, to a private equity firm. Residents say it took their money and let the city rot around them." *The Daily Beast.* Last Modified December 26, 2019. https://www.thedailybeast.com/celebration-florida-how-disneys-community-of-tomorrow-became-a-total-nightmare.

Hourwich, Issac A. "The Evolution of Commercial Law." American Bar Association Journal 1, no. 2 (1915): 70-76.

Inman, Matthew. "Plane." Accessed September 10, 2020. https://theoatmeal. com/comics/plane.

Internal Revenue Service. "Business Structures." Accessed September 9, 2020. https://www.irs.gov/businesses/small-businesses-self-employed/business-structures.

Internal Revenue Service. "Understanding Employee vs. Contractor Designation." Accessed September 9, 2020. https://www.irs.gov/newsroom/ understanding-employee-vs-contractor-designation.

Jimenez, Cesar. "Disney's 'Meet the Robinsons'... a Much Better Tomorrowland Movie." March 9, 2017. https://sciencefactionsite.wordpress. com/2017/03/09/disneys-meet-the-robinsons-a-much-better-tomorrowland-movie/.

Johnson, Kit. "Beauty and the Beast: Disney's Use of the Q and H-1B Visas."

New York University Journal of Law & Liberty 11 (2018): 915-939.

Johnson, Kit. "The Wonderful World of Disney Visas." Florida Law Review 63, no. 4 (2011): 915-958.

Kilkenny, Katie. "Movie Theater Employees Take Aim at Overtime Pay Exemption." *The Hollywood Reporter*. January 6, 2020. https://www.hollywoodreporter.com/news/movie-theater-employees-take-aim-at-overtime-pay-exemption-1270178.

Korkis, Jim. "The 1965 Florida Press Conference." July 4, 2018. https://www.mouseplanet.com/12125/The_1965_Florida_Press_Conference.

Mannheim, Steve. *Walt Disney and the Quest for Community*. New York: Routledge, 2017.

McGrath, James F., "Jesus and the Money Changers (John 2:13-16)." Accessed June, 29, 2020. https://www.bibleodyssey.org:443/en/passages/main-articles/jesus-and-the-moneychangers.

Montilla, Michael Andrew Neil. "Democracy at Disneyworld, How Residents Could Affect Disney's Control Over the Reedy Creek Improvement District." November 17, 2019. https://medium.com/montys-musings/democracy-at-disneyworld-6384baa9bbd5.

Mouse Unleashed. "Disney Housing." October 16, 2018. https://mouseunleashed.com/disney-ip/housing/disney-housing/.

Novak, Lee R. "Market and Feasibility Studies: How to Guide." May 1996. https://pages.uoregon.edu/rgp/PPPM613/downloads/How%20to%20do%20a%20Market%20Analysis.pdf.

Office of Program Policy Analysis & Government Accountability. Central Florida's Reedy Creek Improvement District Has Wide-Ranging Authority. Report No. 04-81, December 2004. http://edocs.dlis.state.fl.us/fldocs/leg/oppaga/2004/0481rpt.pdf.

Parker, Richard. "Related Cases in Commercial Speech." In The First Amendment Encyclopedia. Middle Tennessee State University, 2009. https://www.mtsu.edu/first-amendment/article/212/valentine-v-chrestensen.

Parkinson, Michael G., Daradirek Ekachai, and Laurel Traynowicz Hetherington. "Public Relations Law." In *Handbook of Public Relations*, edited by Robert L. Heath, 247-257. Thousand Oaks, CA: SAGE Publications, Inc., 2001. doi: 10.4135/9781452220727.n18.

Patches, Matt. "Inside Walt Disney's Ambitious, Failed Plan to Build the City of Tomorrow." *Esquire*. May 20, 2015. https://www.esquire.com/entertainment/news/a35104/walt-disney-epcot-history-city-of-tomorrow/.

Pedicini, Sandra. "Disney World's Golden Oak neighborhood draws more permanent residents." *Orlando Sentinel*. September 3, 2016. https://www.orlandosentinel.com/travel/attractions/the-daily-disney/os-disney-world-golden-oak-homes-20160902-story.html.

Public Broadcasting Service. "Slavery by Another Name." Accessed September 10, 2020. https://www.pbs.org/tpt/slavery-by-another-name/themes/company-towns/.

Reedy Creek Improvement District. "Governing, Operating & Maintaining the Most Magical Special Taxing District on Earth." Georgia Engineers Summer Conference. June 8, 2019. https://chambermaster.blob.core.windows.net/userfiles/UserFiles/chambers/9088/CMS/2019_Summer_Conference/Speaker_PPT/2019-06-08-District-Overview-John-Classe.pdf.

Reedy Creek Improvement District. "Reedy Creek Improvement District Comprehensive Plan 2020." October 7, 2010. https://www.rcid.org/wp-content/uploads/2015/06/2020_Comprehensive_Plan.pdf.

Roddenberry, Gene. "When Gene Roddenberry Explained 'Star Trek' in 1966." *The Hollywood Reporter*. September 4, 2018. https://www.hollywoodreporter.com/news/gene-roddenberry-explained-star-trek-1966-1092983.

Rojas, James. "Why Urban Planners Should Work With Artists." April 7, 2015. https://www.kcet.org/shows/artbound/why-urban-planners-should-work-with-artists.

Sachs, Stephen E. "From St. Ives to Cyberspace: The Modern Distortion of the Medieval 'Law Merchant'." *American University International Law Review* 21(2006): 686-812.

Sciretta, Peter. "Brad Bird 'Tomorrowland' Interview: 'The Iron Giant' Blu-Ray, Epcot, NASA, Space Mountain, 'Incredibles 2' and Disneyland." May 20, 2015. https://www.slashfilm.com/brad-bird-tomorrowland-interview/2/.

Slanski, Kathryn E. "The Law of Hammurabi and Its Audience." *Yale Journal of Law & the Humanities* 24, no. 1 (2012): 97-110.

Sotto, Eddie. "COVID 19: What would Walt Disney do?" June 1, 2020. https://blooloop.com/what-would-walt-disney-do-covid-19/.

Simkin, John. "Paul Helliwell." In Spartacus Educational. Last Modified January 2020. https://spartacus-educational.com/JFKhelliwell.htm.

Spence, Jack. "Golden Oak." June 18, 2012. https://allears.net/2012/06/18/golden-oak/.

Stanford University. "The Martin Luther King, Jr. Research and Education Institute." Accessed September 10, 2020. https://kinginstitute.stanford.edu/.

Stark, Michelle. "8 facts about Walt Disney World's luxury Golden Oak neighborhood." Tampa Bay Times. April 24, 2019. https://www.tampabay.com/florida/2019/04/24/8-facts-about-walt-disney-worlds-luxury-golden-oak-neighborhood/.

Suarez, Nestor. "Glen Curtiss – A Look Back at the Elon Musk and Steve Jobs of the early 1900s." May 20, 2018. http://new.miamisprings.com/glenn-curtiss-a-look-back-at-the-elon-musk-and-steve-jobs-of-the-early-1900s/.

"Rescuing Celebration." Accessed September 10, 2020. https://cookiekelly-blog.com/.

The Disney Movie Review. "The Dream of EPCOT fulfilled in 'Tomorrowland'." Accessed September 10, 2020. http://www.thedisneymoviereview.com/the-dream-of-epcot-fulfilled-in-tomorrowland/.

The Mouselets. "The Abandoned Walt Disney World Airport." September 20, 2018. https://themouselets.com/the-abandoned-walt-disney-world-airport.

The Walt Disney Company. "10 Wild Facts Behind Walt Disney World Resort's Conservation Efforts." Accessed September 10, 2020. https://disneyrewards.com/blog/travel-parks/10-wild-facts-behind-walt-disney-world-resorts-conservation-efforts/#:~:text=Nearly%201%2F3%20of%20Walt,their%20young%20before%20flying%20more.

The Walt Disney Company. "Disney Careers: Housing Information." Accessed September 9, 2020. https://jobs.disneycareers.com/housing-information.

The Walt Disney Company. "Donald in Mathmagicland (film)." Accessed September 10, 2020. https://d23.com/a-to-z/donald-in-mathmagic-land-film/.

The Walt Disney Company. "Golden Oak at Walt Disney World Resort." Accessed September 10, 2020. https://www.disneygoldenoak.com/news-updates/#!2.

Tierney, T.F. *Intelligent Infrastructure: Zip Cars, Invisible Networks, and Urban Transformation.* Charlottesville: University of Virginia Press, 2017.

Trashcans Unlimited. "Garbage Collection at Walt Disney World: What the Magic Kingdom Can Teach You about Waste Management." August 14, 2018. https://trashcansunlimited.com/blog/garbage-collection-at-walt-disney-world-what-the-magic-kingdom-can-teach-you-about-waste-management/.

Turner, Gregg M. *The Florida Land Boom of the 1920s.* Jefferson: McFarland & Company, Inc., 2015.

Turner, Tom. "Geoffrey Jellicoe urban landscape design for Motopia housing." July 4, 2016. http://www.landscapearchitecture.org.uk/geoffrey-jellicoe-urban-landscape-design-for-motopia-housing/.

United States Department of Defense. DoD News Briefing - Secretary

Rumsfeld and Gen. Myers. Accessed September 9, 2020. https://archive.
defense.gov/Transcripts/Transcript.aspx?TranscriptID=2636

United States Department of State. Foreign Consular Offices in the United
States 1969. The Ohio State University. Digitized Aug 31, 2017.

University of Miami. "Bernhardt E. Muller collection." Accessed September
10, 2020. https://atom.library.miami.edu/asm0655.

"Walt Disney's original E.P.C.O.T film (1966) HD RESTORED SHORT
VERSION." YouTube video, 19:53 min. Extract from a larger project.
Posted by The Original EPCOT. https://www.youtube.com/watch?v=r9d-
2FEAR2t4#action=share.

Watson, Vanessa. "African Urban Fantasies: Dreams or Nightmares?" *Environment and Urbanization* 26, no. 1 (2014): 215–231.

Weiss, Werner. An Urban Legend about Disney's Contemporary. April 23,
2010. https://www.yesterland.com/contemporary.html.

"Welcome to Celebration." Accessed September 10, 2020. https://celebration.
fl.us/.

World Architecture Community. "Project." Accessed September 10, 2020.
https://worldarchitecture.org/wa-top-teaser/cph/project.

Worstall, Tim. "Star Trek Economics Is Just True Communism Arriving." Forbes. October 5, 2015. https://www.forbes.com/sites/tim-
worstall/2015/10/05/star-trek-economics-is-just-true-communism-arriv-
ing/#3b26204aef64.

Zarniwoop. "Dlp=EPCOT?" Micechat the Happiest Place in Cyberspace.
September 7, 2010. https://discuss.micechat.com/forum/disney-theme-
park-news-and-discussion/disneyland-paris/146845-dlp-epcot.

About the Author

Richard A.C. Alton has a decade and half of legal experience and served more than 6 years as an assistant college professor teaching business law & ethics. Alton is one of few legal scholars that is not an active full-time professor. Alton maintains a strong network, as he is the founder of the Society for Independent Legal Authorship and served as the Past Chair for the Florida Bar International Law Section's Committee on Public International Law, Human Rights & Global Justice.

Alton's scholarly work includes five law review pieces that have been published by journals out of well-known institutions such as the University of Miami, Michigan State University, and Tulane. Additionally, his work has the honor of being cited as authoritative by the second highest court in America, the United States Circuit Court of Appeals. His work has been referenced in publications and by authors across Europe, Africa, the United States, and Canada, even reaching as far as Indonesia. Alton's practical guides have appeared in publications like the International Law Quarterly and the Commentator, and help generate a further interest in his work as well increasing the core audience.

Alton currently lives in South Florida with his wife, Melissa, their three children, and bulldog Lupin.

www.ingramcontent.com/pod-product-compliance
Lightning Source LLC
Chambersburg PA
CBHW020155200326
41521CB00006B/381